LangFlow in Action

A Hands-On Guide to Building Agentic Workflows and Retrieval-Augmented Generation Applications"

©

Written By

Morgan Devline

Table of Contents

Chapter 1: Introduction

LangFlow is a groundbreaking tool that empowers developers, data scientists, and AI enthusiasts to design, visualize, and deploy workflows for **Large Language Models (LLMs)**. This introduction provides an overview of LangFlow, explores its significance in the rise of **Agentic Workflows** and **Retrieval-Augmented Generation (RAG)** in AI, and explains how LangFlow simplifies workflow design. We'll also identify the key audience for this book and how they can benefit from mastering LangFlow.

1.1   An Overview of LangFlow and its Ecosystem

LangFlow is a visual interface that enables users to create and manage workflows involving LLMs, such as OpenAI's GPT models or similar frameworks. With LangFlow, users can connect tools, knowledge bases, APIs, and LLMs into cohesive pipelines that execute complex tasks like question answering, content generation, or multi-agent coordination.

Key Features of LangFlow

- **Drag-and-Drop Interface**: Simplifies workflow creation by allowing users to visually connect components.

- **Integration with LangChain**: LangFlow builds upon LangChain, a popular framework for building LLM-powered applications.

- **Customizability**: Users can add custom plugins, tools, and configurations to tailor workflows to specific use cases.

- **Scalability**: Supports workflows ranging from simple prototypes to enterprise-grade applications.

Core Components of the Ecosystem

Component	Description
Nodes	Building blocks representing actions like input capture, retrieval, or generation.
Edges	Connections between nodes that define data flow in the pipeline.
LLMs	Large Language Models for generating text, summarization, and more.
Knowledge Bases	Databases or vector stores used for retrieval-augmented workflows.
APIs and Tools	External integrations, such as search engines, data fetchers, or CRMs.

LangFlow bridges the gap between raw AI capabilities and practical, deployable solutions, making it a valuable tool in the AI ecosystem.

1.2 The Rise of Agentic Workflows and RAG in AI
What are Agentic Workflows?

Agentic workflows refer to systems where AI agents autonomously perform tasks, make decisions, and interact with tools or data sources. These workflows combine multiple steps, such as retrieving information, processing data, and generating outputs, into a seamless operation.

What is RAG (Retrieval-Augmented Generation)?

RAG enhances AI's capabilities by combining:

- **Knowledge Retrieval**: Fetching relevant data from external sources like vector stores or knowledge bases.

- **Language Generation**: Using LLMs to generate responses based on the retrieved information.

Why are These Concepts Revolutionary?

1. **Enhanced Accuracy**:
   - By incorporating external knowledge, RAG reduces the risk of hallucinations in LLM-generated responses.

2. **Dynamic Problem Solving**:
   - Agentic workflows allow AI to adapt to complex scenarios and execute multi-step tasks autonomously.

3. **Real-World Applications**:
   - Examples include intelligent chatbots, research assistants, and automated customer support.

LangFlow's Role in This Revolution

LangFlow enables users to:

- Design agentic workflows by connecting nodes for decision-making, retrieval, and generation.

- Build RAG applications with integrated retrieval nodes and LLMs.

- Focus on innovation by eliminating technical complexities in workflow development.

1.3 How LangFlow Simplifies Workflow Design

LangFlow stands out by providing a user-friendly platform for creating AI workflows without requiring extensive programming expertise. Here's how it achieves this:

1. Visual Workflow Design

LangFlow's drag-and-drop interface allows users to:

- Add nodes for input, processing, and output.

- Connect these nodes with edges to define data flow.

- Visually debug workflows to ensure accuracy.

2. Seamless Integration with Tools

LangFlow supports integration with:

- **Vector Stores**: For knowledge retrieval in RAG applications.

- **APIs**: For external data fetching or live updates.

- **Custom Scripts**: To extend functionality beyond built-in tools.

3. Customizable and Modular Workflows

Users can:

- Configure each node's parameters (e.g., LLM temperature, token limits).

- Save and reuse workflows as templates for similar projects.

4. Debugging and Monitoring

LangFlow provides built-in tools for:

- Monitoring data flow between nodes.

- Debugging errors in real-time.

- Optimizing performance for faster and more accurate results.

5. Scalability

LangFlow's workflows can scale from local prototypes to enterprise-grade solutions by integrating cloud-based resources and APIs.

1.4 Who Should Read This Book?

This book is designed for a broad audience, from beginners exploring AI workflows to seasoned professionals looking to optimize LLM applications. Here's a breakdown of who will benefit:

1. Developers

- **Needs**: Practical tools for building AI-driven applications.

- **How This Book Helps**: Offers step-by-step tutorials and code examples to integrate LangFlow into projects.

2. Data Scientists

- **Needs**: Tools to process and analyze data using AI.
- **How This Book Helps**: Explains how to design RAG pipelines for data retrieval and summarization.

3. AI Enthusiasts

- **Needs**: A gateway to understanding and leveraging LLM workflows.
- **How This Book Helps**: Provides a beginner-friendly introduction to LangFlow and its ecosystem.

4. Business Professionals

- **Needs**: AI solutions for automation and decision-making.
- **How This Book Helps**: Demonstrates real-world use cases like customer support bots and research assistants.

5. Educators and Researchers

- **Needs**: Simplified tools to teach or conduct experiments with AI.
- **How This Book Helps**: Showcases practical workflows that can be adapted for academic or training purposes.

What You Will Learn

By the end of this book, readers will:

- Understand the basics of LangFlow and its integration with LLMs.
- Build simple and advanced workflows, including RAG pipelines and agentic systems.
- Gain the confidence to apply LangFlow in real-world scenarios.

LangFlow is more than a tool—it's a gateway to creating intelligent, adaptable, and scalable AI workflows. This book will guide you step-by-step to mastering LangFlow and unlocking the full potential of LLMs and RAG applications. Let's dive in!

Chapter: 2 The Power of Agentic Workflows and Retrieval-Augmented Generation

2.1 What are Agentic Workflows?
Definition

Agentic workflows are advanced systems that use **autonomous agents** to manage and execute tasks, enabling seamless automation, decision-making, and dynamic interactions. In the context of LangFlow, these workflows allow users to design intelligent pipelines where agents independently act upon data, collaborate with other agents or tools, and adapt to changing requirements.

Key Characteristics of Agentic Workflows

1. **Autonomy**: Agents can operate without constant human intervention, handling complex tasks independently.

2. **Dynamic Interaction**: They communicate with other agents, tools, or systems in real-time.

3. **Decision-Making**: Agents are capable of making logical decisions based on the data they process.

4. **Task-Oriented Design**: Workflows are structured to achieve specific outcomes, such as answering queries, processing data, or automating operations.

How LangFlow Enables Agentic Workflows

LangFlow provides an intuitive interface to:

- Define agents and their roles in workflows.

- Set up interactions between agents and tools.

- Monitor and debug the behavior of agents within a workflow.

Examples of Agentic Workflows

Example 1: Customer Support Automation

- **Agents Involved**: FAQ retrieval agent, sentiment analysis agent, escalation agent.

- **Workflow**: A customer question is received and passed to the FAQ retrieval agent. If no answer is found, the sentiment analysis agent determines the tone of the query and escalates the issue to the relevant support team.

- **Outcome**: Faster and more accurate resolution of customer issues.

Example 2: Research Assistant Workflow

- **Agents Involved**: Query agent, summarization agent, citation agent.

- **Workflow**: A user submits a query. The query agent retrieves relevant academic papers, the summarization agent extracts key information, and the citation agent provides references.

- **Outcome**: Streamlined research with accurate summaries and references.

Example 3: Multi-Agent Content Generation

- **Agents Involved**: Content retrieval agent, grammar-check agent, SEO optimization agent.

- **Workflow**: The content retrieval agent gathers relevant information. The grammar-check agent refines the text, and the SEO agent optimizes it for search engines.

- **Outcome**: High-quality, SEO-friendly content with minimal human intervention.

Benefits of Agentic Workflows

1. **Increased Efficiency**:
    - Automates repetitive tasks, saving time and resources.

2. **Scalability**:

   o Handles large volumes of tasks without degradation in performance.

3. **Adaptability**:

   o Adjusts dynamically to new inputs or conditions.

4. **Enhanced Collaboration**:

   o Multiple agents can work together to complete complex workflows.

5. **Error Reduction**:

   o Automation reduces the likelihood of human error.

2.2 The Concept of RAG: Knowledge Retrieval Meets Generation
Definition

Retrieval-Augmented Generation (RAG) is a methodology that combines the capabilities of large language models (LLMs) with external knowledge retrieval systems. It allows the LLM to provide accurate and context-aware responses by incorporating relevant information from knowledge bases or vector stores.

How RAG Works

1. **Query Input**: The user inputs a query.

2. **Knowledge Retrieval**:

   o The system retrieves relevant information from a database, API, or vector store.

3. **Response Generation**:

   o The retrieved information is used as context for the LLM to generate a detailed and accurate response.

Key Components of RAG

1. **LLMs**: Models like GPT process the user's query and generate responses.

2. **Knowledge Bases or Vector Stores**: Store structured or unstructured data for retrieval.

3. **Retrieval Systems**: Mechanisms to fetch relevant data based on the user's query.

Benefits of RAG

- **Improved Accuracy**:
  - Responses are grounded in factual data.

- **Reduced Hallucination**:
  - LLMs rely on verified information rather than speculative generation.

- **Real-Time Updates**:
  - RAG workflows can incorporate the latest data from dynamic sources.

- **Customizability**:
  - Allows domain-specific knowledge to be embedded into workflows.

Example Workflow: Building a RAG System in LangFlow

Workflow Steps:

1. **Input Node**:
   - User submits a query (e.g., "What are the latest advancements in AI?").

2. **Retrieval Node**:
   - Fetches relevant articles from a knowledge base.

3. **LLM Node**:

o Combines the retrieved data with the query to generate a response.

4. **Output Node**:

o Displays the final response.

Code Example:

```
from langchain.chains import RetrievalQA
from langchain.vectorstores import FAISS
from langchain.llms import OpenAI

# Set up a vector store (e.g., FAISS)
vector_store = FAISS.load_local("path/to/vectorstore")

# Set up the LLM
llm = OpenAI(model="gpt-4")

# Create a RAG workflow
rag_chain = RetrievalQA(llm=llm, retriever=vector_store.as_retriever())

# Query the system
query = "What are the latest advancements in AI?"
response = rag_chain.run(query)
print(response)
```

Challenges in RAG

- **Data Quality**:

  o Low-quality knowledge bases can lead to poor responses.

- **Latency**:

  o Real-time retrieval can introduce delays.

- **Integration Complexity**:

  o Combining LLMs with external systems requires careful configuration.

2.3 Real-World Applications for LangFlow

LangFlow excels in enabling practical implementations of agentic workflows and RAG across various industries. Below are some real-world use cases:

1. Customer Support Systems

- **Application**: Automating customer queries with RAG workflows.

- **Example**:

  o Retrieve answers from a knowledge base.

  o Use sentiment analysis to prioritize support tickets.

- **Benefit**: Improves response times and customer satisfaction.

2. Research Assistants

- **Application**: Streamlining academic research.

- **Example**:

  o Summarize research papers.

  o Provide citations and context for findings.

- **Benefit**: Speeds up the research process with accurate data.

3. Legal Document Processing

- **Application**: Automating the retrieval of legal precedents and document analysis.

- **Example**:

  o Fetch relevant case studies.

  o Generate summaries of legal documents.

- **Benefit**: Reduces manual effort and improves accuracy.

4. Content Creation

- **Application**: Enhancing the efficiency of content generation workflows.

- **Example**:
  - Generate blog posts optimized for SEO.
  - Use RAG to incorporate the latest trends and data.
- **Benefit**: Produces high-quality, context-aware content quickly.

5. Healthcare Applications

- **Application**: Supporting medical professionals with accurate information retrieval.
- **Example**:
  - Retrieve clinical guidelines and research papers.
  - Generate patient-friendly explanations.
- **Benefit**: Enhances decision-making and patient care.

Agentic workflows and RAG represent transformative advances in AI, enabling systems to operate autonomously, retrieve accurate data, and generate context-aware responses. LangFlow serves as a powerful platform to design, implement, and optimize these workflows, unlocking endless possibilities across industries.

Chapter:2 The Power of Agentic Workflows and Retrieval-Augmented Generation

2.1 What are Agentic Workflows?
Definition

Agentic workflows are advanced systems that use **autonomous agents** to manage and execute tasks, enabling seamless automation, decision-making, and dynamic interactions. In the context of LangFlow, these workflows allow users to design intelligent pipelines where agents independently act upon data, collaborate with other agents or tools, and adapt to changing requirements.

Key Characteristics of Agentic Workflows

1. **Autonomy**: Agents can operate without constant human intervention, handling complex tasks independently.

2. **Dynamic Interaction**: They communicate with other agents, tools, or systems in real-time.

3. **Decision-Making**: Agents are capable of making logical decisions based on the data they process.

4. **Task-Oriented Design**: Workflows are structured to achieve specific outcomes, such as answering queries, processing data, or automating operations.

How LangFlow Enables Agentic Workflows

LangFlow provides an intuitive interface to:

- Define agents and their roles in workflows.

- Set up interactions between agents and tools.

- Monitor and debug the behavior of agents within a workflow.

Examples of Agentic Workflows

Example 1: Customer Support Automation

- **Agents Involved**: FAQ retrieval agent, sentiment analysis agent, escalation agent.

- **Workflow**: A customer question is received and passed to the FAQ retrieval agent. If no answer is found, the sentiment analysis agent determines the tone of the query and escalates the issue to the relevant support team.

- **Outcome**: Faster and more accurate resolution of customer issues.

Example 2: Research Assistant Workflow

- **Agents Involved**: Query agent, summarization agent, citation agent.

- **Workflow**: A user submits a query. The query agent retrieves relevant academic papers, the summarization agent extracts key information, and the citation agent provides references.

- **Outcome**: Streamlined research with accurate summaries and references.

Example 3: Multi-Agent Content Generation

- **Agents Involved**: Content retrieval agent, grammar-check agent, SEO optimization agent.

- **Workflow**: The content retrieval agent gathers relevant information. The grammar-check agent refines the text, and the SEO agent optimizes it for search engines.

- **Outcome**: High-quality, SEO-friendly content with minimal human intervention.

Benefits of Agentic Workflows

1. **Increased Efficiency**:
   - Automates repetitive tasks, saving time and resources.

2. **Scalability**:

    o   Handles large volumes of tasks without degradation in performance.

3. **Adaptability**:

    o   Adjusts dynamically to new inputs or conditions.

4. **Enhanced Collaboration**:

    o   Multiple agents can work together to complete complex workflows.

5. **Error Reduction**:

    o   Automation reduces the likelihood of human error.

2.2 The Concept of RAG
Definition

Retrieval-Augmented Generation (RAG) is a methodology that combines the capabilities of large language models (LLMs) with external knowledge retrieval systems. It allows the LLM to provide accurate and context-aware responses by incorporating relevant information from knowledge bases or vector stores.

How RAG Works

1. **Query Input**: The user inputs a query.

2. **Knowledge Retrieval**:

    o   The system retrieves relevant information from a database, API, or vector store.

3. **Response Generation**:

    o   The retrieved information is used as context for the LLM to generate a detailed and accurate response.

Key Components of RAG

1. **LLMs**: Models like GPT process the user's query and generate responses.

2. **Knowledge Bases or Vector Stores**: Store structured or unstructured data for retrieval.

3. **Retrieval Systems**: Mechanisms to fetch relevant data based on the user's query.

Benefits of RAG

- **Improved Accuracy**:

  o Responses are grounded in factual data.

- **Reduced Hallucination**:

  o LLMs rely on verified information rather than speculative generation.

- **Real-Time Updates**:

  o RAG workflows can incorporate the latest data from dynamic sources.

- **Customizability**:

  o Allows domain-specific knowledge to be embedded into workflows.

Example Workflow: Building a RAG System in LangFlow

Workflow Steps:

1. **Input Node**:

   o User submits a query (e.g., "What are the latest advancements in AI?").

2. **Retrieval Node**:

   o Fetches relevant articles from a knowledge base.

3. **LLM Node**:

   o Combines the retrieved data with the query to generate a response.

4. **Output Node**:

   o Displays the final response.

Code Example:

```
from langchain.chains import RetrievalQA
from langchain.vectorstores import FAISS
from langchain.llms import OpenAI

# Set up a vector store (e.g., FAISS)
vector_store = FAISS.load_local("path/to/vectorstore")

# Set up the LLM
llm = OpenAI(model="gpt-4")

# Create a RAG workflow
rag_chain = RetrievalQA(llm=llm, retriever=vector_store.as_retriever())

# Query the system
query = "What are the latest advancements in AI?"
response = rag_chain.run(query)
print(response)
```

Challenges in RAG

- **Data Quality**:
    - Low-quality knowledge bases can lead to poor responses.

- **Latency**:
    - Real-time retrieval can introduce delays.

- **Integration Complexity**:
    - Combining LLMs with external systems requires careful configuration.

2.3 Real-World Applications for LangFlow

LangFlow excels in enabling practical implementations of agentic workflows and RAG across various industries. Below are some real-world use cases:

1. Customer Support Systems

- **Application**: Automating customer queries with RAG workflows.

- **Example**:
    - Retrieve answers from a knowledge base.
    - Use sentiment analysis to prioritize support tickets.

- **Benefit**: Improves response times and customer satisfaction.

2. Research Assistants

- **Application**: Streamlining academic research.

- **Example**:
    - Summarize research papers.
    - Provide citations and context for findings.

- **Benefit**: Speeds up the research process with accurate data.

3. Legal Document Processing

- **Application**: Automating the retrieval of legal precedents and document analysis.

- **Example**:
    - Fetch relevant case studies.
    - Generate summaries of legal documents.

- **Benefit**: Reduces manual effort and improves accuracy.

4. Content Creation

- **Application**: Enhancing the efficiency of content generation workflows.

- **Example**:
    - Generate blog posts optimized for SEO.
    - Use RAG to incorporate the latest trends and data.

- **Benefit**: Produces high-quality, context-aware content quickly.

5. Healthcare Applications

- **Application**: Supporting medical professionals with accurate information retrieval.

- **Example**:

  o Retrieve clinical guidelines and research papers.

  o Generate patient-friendly explanations.

- **Benefit**: Enhances decision-making and patient care.

Agentic workflows and RAG represent transformative advances in AI, enabling systems to operate autonomously, retrieve accurate data, and generate context-aware responses. LangFlow serves as a powerful platform to design, implement, and optimize these workflows, unlocking endless possibilities across industries.

Chapter 3: Setting Up LangFlow

3.1 Installation and Configuration

Getting Started with LangFlow

LangFlow is a powerful tool that simplifies the creation and management of workflows involving Large Language Models (LLMs). To use it effectively, proper installation and configuration are essential.

System Requirements

Before installing LangFlow, ensure your system meets the following requirements:

- **Operating System**: Windows, macOS, or Linux.

- **Python Version**: Python 3.8 or higher.

- **RAM**: At least 8GB (16GB or higher recommended for larger workflows).

- **Disk Space**: At least 1GB of free space.

Step-by-Step Installation Guide

Step 1: Install Python

Ensure you have Python installed on your system. You can download it from python.org.

- Verify the installation:

```
python --version
```

Step 2: Set Up a Virtual Environment

It is recommended to use a virtual environment to avoid dependency conflicts.

- Create a virtual environment:

```
python -m venv langflow_env
```

- Activate the virtual environment:

       o   On Windows:

.\langflow_env\Scripts\activate

       o   On macOS/Linux:

source langflow_env/bin/activate

Step 3: Install LangFlow

Use pip to install LangFlow and its dependencies.

pip install langflow

Step 4: Launch LangFlow

Once installed, launch LangFlow using the following command:

langflow

This command starts the LangFlow server, and you can access the interface via a web browser at http://localhost:8000.

Step 5: Optional Dependencies

For advanced features, you may need additional packages such as vector stores or specific API integrations. These can be installed as needed.

Feature	Required Package
Vector Store Support	faiss, pinecone
API Integrations	requests, openai

3.2 Understanding LangFlow's Interface
Overview of the LangFlow Interface

The LangFlow interface is designed to be intuitive, allowing users to visually design workflows with minimal coding. Below is a breakdown of the interface's key components.

1. Main Dashboard

The dashboard is the starting point of LangFlow and contains:

- **New Workflow**: Create a new workflow from scratch.

- **Existing Workflows**: Access and edit previously saved workflows.

- **Templates**: Pre-configured workflows for common use cases.

2. Workflow Designer

The workflow designer is where you create and manage workflows. It has the following elements:

- **Canvas**: The central area where nodes are placed and connected.

- **Toolbar**: A set of tools for adding, editing, and deleting nodes.

- **Properties Panel**: Displays configuration options for the selected node.

Element	Description
Canvas	Drag and drop nodes to design workflows.
Toolbar	Includes tools for adding nodes, edges, and other elements.
Properties	Configure specific settings for each node or connection.

3. Node Library

A library of pre-built nodes is available, categorized by functionality:

- **LLMs**: Nodes for language models like OpenAI GPT.

- **Memory**: Nodes to manage context and retain information.

- **Tools**: Nodes for APIs, file I/O, and other integrations.

- **Data Flow**: Nodes for handling data transformations and routing.

4. Output and Logs

- **Output Panel**: Displays the results of workflow executions.

- **Logs**: Provides detailed information for debugging and optimization.

3.3 Introduction to Nodes, Edges, and Data Flow

1. Nodes

Nodes are the building blocks of LangFlow workflows. Each node represents a specific task or function.

Types of Nodes

1. **Input Nodes**:

   o Capture user inputs, such as text queries.

   o Example: A text input node for user questions.

2. **Processing Nodes**:

   o Perform tasks such as calling an API, running an LLM, or performing calculations.

   o Example: An LLM node for generating text.

3. **Output Nodes**:

   o Display or return the final result of the workflow.

   o Example: A display node to show generated responses.

Node Configuration

Each node has configurable properties such as input types, output types, and operational parameters. For instance:

- An LLM node may have properties like:

   o **Temperature**: Controls the randomness of responses.

   o **Max Tokens**: Limits the length of responses.

2. Edges

Edges connect nodes, defining the flow of data between them.

- **Directional Arrows**: Indicate the direction of data flow.
- **Validation**: Ensure compatible data types are passed between nodes.

Example Workflow

1. Input Node ➜ User enters a question.
2. Retrieval Node ➜ Fetch relevant data.
3. LLM Node ➜ Generate a response based on the retrieved data.
4. Output Node ➜ Display the response to the user.

3. Data Flow

Data flow represents how information moves through the workflow, from input to output.

Key Concepts

1. **Sequential Execution**:
   - Data flows in the order defined by the connections.
2. **Parallel Processing**:
   - Multiple nodes can operate simultaneously if their inputs are independent.
3. **Transformations**:
   - Data can be modified as it moves through nodes using built-in functions or custom logic.

Example Data Flow

1. **Input**: User asks, "What is LangFlow?"
2. **Processing**:
   - Retrieval Node fetches relevant information.
   - LLM Node generates a comprehensive explanation.

3. **Output**: "LangFlow is a tool for building AI workflows."

By the end of this chapter, you will have installed LangFlow, understood its interface, and gained a foundational understanding of nodes, edges, and data flow. These skills will prepare you for building more complex workflows in subsequent chapters.

Chapter 4: Creating Your First Workflow

4.1 Building a Simple RAG Pipeline
Introduction to RAG Pipelines

A **Retrieval-Augmented Generation (RAG)** pipeline combines knowledge retrieval and language generation to produce accurate, context-aware results. In this section, we will build a simple RAG pipeline in LangFlow, guiding you step-by-step through the process.

Steps to Build a RAG Pipeline

Step 1: Define the Problem

- **Objective**: Create a system where users can query a knowledge base (e.g., for FAQs or research papers), and the system retrieves relevant information to generate an insightful response.

Step 2: Set Up LangFlow

1. Install LangFlow using the following command:

pip install langflow

2. Launch the LangFlow interface:

langflow

3. Open the web-based LangFlow interface in your browser.

Step 3: Design the Workflow

1. **Input Node**:

    o Add a node to capture user input (e.g., a question).

2. **Retrieval Node**:

    o Connect a retrieval tool (e.g., vector store) to fetch relevant information.

3. **LLM Node**:

    o Link the retrieval node to an LLM (e.g., OpenAI GPT) to generate a detailed response.

4. **Output Node**:

    o Display the final response to the user.

Step 4: Configure the Components

- **Vector Store**:

    o Upload your data (e.g., knowledge base) into a vector store like FAISS.

- **LLM**:

    o Select a language model and adjust parameters like temperature for generation quality.

Step 5: Run the Pipeline

- Test the workflow with various inputs to ensure relevant retrieval and coherent responses.

Example RAG Workflow in LangFlow

1. **User Input**: "What are the benefits of AI in healthcare?"

2. **Retrieval**: Fetches relevant articles or summaries about AI in healthcare from a vector store.

3. **LLM Response**: Generates a response like: "AI in healthcare offers benefits such as improved diagnostics, personalized treatment, and operational efficiency."

4.2 Key Elements: LLMs, Tools, and Memory
1. Large Language Models (LLMs)

- **Role**: The core engine for processing user queries and generating responses.

- **Common LLMs**:

- o OpenAI GPT models.
- o Google's T5 models.

- **Key Configurations**:
  - o **Temperature**: Controls randomness of responses.
  - o **Max Tokens**: Limits response length.

2. Tools

- **Definition**: External components that enhance workflow capabilities.
- **Examples**:
  - o APIs for fetching live data.
  - o Custom scripts for processing specific tasks.
- **Integration in LangFlow**:
  - o Drag-and-drop tools into workflows.
  - o Configure input/output connections.

3. Memory

- **Purpose**: Maintains context between user interactions for dynamic, multi-turn conversations.
- **Types**:
  - o **Short-Term Memory**: For single session queries.
  - o **Long-Term Memory**: Stores user preferences or past interactions.
- **Configuration in LangFlow**:
  - o Add a memory node to workflows.
  - o Connect memory to the LLM for enhanced context retention.

4.3 Testing and Debugging Basics

Importance of Testing

Testing ensures your workflows operate as intended, delivering accurate results and handling edge cases effectively.

Key Testing Strategies

1. **Unit Testing**:

   o   Test individual nodes (e.g., LLM or retrieval).

2. **End-to-End Testing**:

   o   Run the complete workflow with sample inputs to ensure smooth data flow.

Debugging in LangFlow

LangFlow offers built-in tools to help debug workflows efficiently.

Debugging Steps:

1. **Monitor Node Logs**:

   o   Check logs for each node to identify errors.

2. **Token Usage Analysis**:

   o   Ensure your workflow doesn't exceed token limits.

3. **Validation Tests**:

   o   Verify data format and type consistency between nodes.

Common Issues and Fixes

Issue	Cause	Solution
Missing Data in Retrieval	Incorrect query or poorly indexed data	Optimize vector store indexing
Unintelligible LLM Responses	Improper prompt or high temperature	Refine prompt and adjust parameters

Workflow Crashes	Misconfigured node connections	Recheck node connections and settings

Example Debugging Scenario

Problem: The workflow outputs irrelevant responses.
Debugging:

1. Check if the retrieval node fetches correct data.

2. Refine the LLM prompt to ensure clarity.

3. Test with different inputs and validate improvements.

By the end of this chapter, you will have a functional RAG pipeline and a solid understanding of the foundational elements needed to design and debug LangFlow workflows.

Chapter 5: Agentic Workflow Design

5.1 Understanding Agents in LangFlow
What are Agents?

Agents in LangFlow are autonomous components that act on behalf of users to achieve specific tasks by interacting with various tools and data sources. They are capable of:

- Interpreting user inputs.

- Making decisions based on predefined logic.

- Generating outputs by leveraging tools such as APIs, databases, and large language models (LLMs).

Why Use Agents?

Agents simplify complex workflows by automating decision-making and task execution. They can:

- Handle multi-step operations without user intervention.

- Dynamically adapt to changes in input or context.

- Enable scalable, modular workflows.

Core Components of an Agent

- **Input Processor**: Understands and interprets user queries.

- **Decision Engine**: Determines the appropriate action based on logic or prompts.

- **Output Generator**: Produces results, often by integrating LLMs or external APIs.

Example Use Case

A customer support chatbot acting as an agent:

1. **Input:** User asks, "How do I reset my password?"

2. **Decision**: The agent determines the correct FAQ entry or initiates a password reset API.

3. **Output**: The agent provides step-by-step guidance or sends a reset link.

5.2 Multi-Agent Systems: Communication and Orchestration

What are Multi-Agent Systems?

Multi-agent systems involve multiple agents working together to accomplish complex tasks. Each agent is specialized for a specific role, and they collaborate through communication and orchestration.

Key Characteristics

1. **Specialization**:

   o Each agent focuses on a single task, such as data retrieval, computation, or decision-making.

2. **Coordination**:

   o Agents share data and results to achieve a common goal.

3. **Autonomy**:

   o Agents operate independently but follow defined protocols for collaboration.

Communication Between Agents

LangFlow enables communication between agents through data nodes and edges. Agents can:

- Share intermediate outputs (e.g., retrieved data).

- Trigger actions in other agents (e.g., activating a calculation module).

Orchestration in LangFlow

Orchestration ensures that agents perform their tasks in a logical order. LangFlow achieves this through:

- **Workflow Nodes**: Define the sequence of operations.
- **Conditional Logic**: Guide decision-making based on context or results.

Real-World Example

A research assistant application with multiple agents:

1. **Agent 1**: Retrieves relevant papers from a database.
2. **Agent 2**: Summarizes key findings using an LLM.
3. **Agent 3**: Generates a report with actionable insights.

5.3 Example Project: Building a Conversational Agent
Objective

Create a conversational agent that can answer user queries by retrieving relevant information and providing detailed responses using an LLM.

Steps to Build

Step 1: Define the Workflow

1. **Input**: Capture the user's query.
2. **Retrieval**: Use a vector store to fetch relevant information.
3. **Response Generation**: Use an LLM to craft a detailed answer.

Step 2: Configure LangFlow

1. Open LangFlow and create a new project.
2. Add the following nodes:

- o **Input Node**: Accepts user queries.

- o **Retrieval Node**: Fetches data from a vector store.

- o **LLM Node**: Generates a response based on the retrieved data.

- o **Output Node**: Displays the response to the user.

Step 3: Integrate Components

1. Connect the **Input Node** to the **Retrieval Node**.

2. Link the **Retrieval Node** to the **LLM Node**.

3. Attach the **LLM Node** to the **Output Node**.

Step 4: Test the Agent

- Query: "What are the benefits of renewable energy?"

- Response:

  1. Retrieval: Fetches documents discussing renewable energy benefits.

  2. LLM Output: "Renewable energy reduces carbon emissions, lowers costs, and provides sustainable power sources."

Code Example

python

```
from langflow.core import LangFlow
from langchain.llms import OpenAI
from langchain.vectorstores import FAISS
from langchain.prompts import PromptTemplate

# Initialize LangFlow
flow = LangFlow()
```

```
# Configure LLM
llm = OpenAI(model_name="gpt-3.5-turbo", temperature=0.7)

# Set up vector store for retrieval
vector_store = FAISS.load_local("knowledge_base_index")

# Define prompt template
prompt = PromptTemplate(template="User Query: {query}\nResponse:")

# Build the workflow
flow.add_node("Input", type="text_input")
flow.add_node("Retrieval", type="vector_store", store=vector_store)
flow.add_node("LLM", model=llm, prompt_template=prompt)
flow.add_node("Output", type="text_display")

# Connect nodes
flow.connect("Input", "Retrieval")
flow.connect("Retrieval", "LLM")
flow.connect("LLM", "Output")

# Run the workflow
response = flow.run(input_data="What are the benefits of renewable energy?")
print(response)
```

Testing and Refinements

1. **Test Input Variations**:

    o Provide diverse queries to validate retrieval accuracy
      and response quality.

2. **Optimize LLM Parameters**:

    o Adjust temperature and max tokens for clarity and
      brevity.

3. **Handle Errors**:

o   Add fallback mechanisms for cases where no relevant data is retrieved.

Expected Outcome

By the end of this chapter, readers will have:

- A solid understanding of agents and multi-agent systems in LangFlow.

- Practical experience building and testing a conversational agent.

- Knowledge of best practices for refining agent workflows.

Chapter 6: Retrieval-Augmented Generation (RAG) Basics

6.1 Designing Effective RAG Pipelines

What is a RAG Pipeline?

A **Retrieval-Augmented Generation (RAG)** pipeline is a system that combines:

- **Knowledge Retrieval**: Fetching relevant data from a database or knowledge source.

- **Language Generation**: Using an LLM to process retrieved data and generate a coherent response.

This approach enhances the accuracy and relevance of AI-generated content, making it especially useful for applications requiring context-specific answers.

Key Components of a RAG Pipeline

1. **Input Source**:

   o Captures user queries or requests.

2. **Retriever**:

   o Fetches relevant information from a knowledge base.

3. **LLM**:

   o Processes retrieved data and generates a human-like response.

4. **Output System**:

   o Presents the response to the user in an understandable format.

Best Practices for Designing RAG Pipelines

1. **Optimize Querying**:

   o Use natural language prompts to improve retrieval accuracy.

   o Employ filters to narrow down the results from the knowledge base.

2. **Enhance Data Quality**:

   o Ensure your knowledge base contains up-to-date, relevant, and structured data.

3. **Iterative Testing**:

   o Continuously test and refine your pipeline to handle edge cases effectively.

4. **Consider Workflow Modularity**:

   o Design pipelines with reusable nodes for future flexibility.

Steps to Build a Basic RAG Pipeline

1. **Define the Workflow**:

   o Clarify the purpose of the pipeline (e.g., answering FAQs or summarizing documents).

2. **Select Tools and Components**:

   o Choose an LLM, a vector store, and a user interface for input/output.

3. **Integrate Components in LangFlow**:

   o Use LangFlow's drag-and-drop interface to connect input, retrieval, LLM, and output nodes.

4. **Test the Pipeline**:

   o Use varied inputs to validate the pipeline's ability to retrieve and generate relevant information.

6.2 Connecting Knowledge Bases and Vector Stores

What is a Knowledge Base?

A knowledge base is a repository of information structured for efficient retrieval. Examples include:

- FAQ databases.

- Research papers or articles.

- Product catalogs.

What is a Vector Store?

A **vector store** converts textual data into numerical vectors, enabling fast similarity searches. Tools like FAISS (Facebook AI Similarity Search) are commonly used for this purpose.

Steps to Connect a Knowledge Base to a Vector Store

1. **Preprocess the Data**:

   o Convert raw text into smaller, meaningful chunks.

   o Use tools like NLTK or spaCy for text preprocessing.

2. **Generate Embeddings**:

   o Use pre-trained models like OpenAI's embeddings API or Sentence Transformers to transform text chunks into numerical vectors.

3. **Index the Data**:

   o Store vectors in a vector store for efficient retrieval.

   o Example: Index documents in FAISS.

4. **Set Up Retrieval**:

   o Use similarity search algorithms to find relevant vectors based on a user query.

Code Example: Setting Up a Vector Store

python

```
from langchain.embeddings import OpenAIEmbeddings
from langchain.vectorstores import FAISS

# Sample data
documents = ["AI improves healthcare efficiency", "AI transforms education
systems", "AI enables automation in industries"]

# Generate embeddings
embedding_model = OpenAIEmbeddings()
document_embeddings = [embedding_model.embed(text) for text in documents]

# Create a vector store
vector_store = FAISS.from_embeddings(document_embeddings, documents)

# Save the vector store
vector_store.save_local("knowledge_base_index")
```

Integrating the Vector Store in LangFlow

1. Load the vector store into LangFlow:

python

```
from langchain.vectorstores import FAISS
vector_store = FAISS.load_local("knowledge_base_index")
```

2. Connect the retrieval node to the vector store in LangFlow.

3. Test the integration by querying the vector store.

6.3 Example Project: Creating a Research Assistant

Objective

Develop a research assistant that:

- Accepts user queries.

- Retrieves relevant documents from a knowledge base.

- Summarizes findings using an LLM.

Steps to Build

Step 1: Define the Workflow

1. **Input**:

   o Accept user queries like "Summarize advancements in AI."

2. **Retrieval**:

   o Fetch related articles or sections from a vector store.

3. **Response Generation**:

   o Use an LLM to summarize the retrieved content.

Step 2: Configure LangFlow

1. Add these nodes in the LangFlow interface:

   o **Input Node**: Captures user queries.

   o **Retrieval Node**: Searches the vector store for relevant data.

   o **LLM Node**: Processes retrieved data to generate a summary.

   o **Output Node**: Displays the response.

Step 3: Example Implementation

Code Implementation:

python

```
from langchain.llms import OpenAI
from langchain.vectorstores import FAISS
from langchain.prompts import PromptTemplate

# Load vector store
vector_store = FAISS.load_local("knowledge_base_index")

# Configure LLM
llm = OpenAI(model_name="gpt-3.5-turbo", temperature=0.5)

# Prompt template
prompt_template = PromptTemplate(template="Summarize the following:
{retrieved_content}")

# Querying the vector store
query = "AI in education"
retrieved_content = vector_store.similarity_search(query, top_k=3)

# Generate response
response =
llm.generate(prompt_template.format(retrieved_content=retrieved_content))
print(response)
```

Step 4: Test the Assistant

1. Input query: "Summarize the role of AI in education."

2. Expected Output:

   o "AI in education improves personalization, automates grading, and enhances accessibility."

Step 5: Debugging and Optimization

- **Issue**: Irrelevant documents retrieved.

  o **Solution**: Refine the vector store indexing or adjust query embeddings.

- **Issue**: Long, verbose responses.

- o **Solution**: Modify the LLM's temperature and token settings.

Outcome

By the end of this chapter, readers will:

1. Understand the fundamentals of RAG pipelines.

2. Learn how to connect knowledge bases and vector stores.

3. Build a functional research assistant, leveraging retrieval and generation capabilities effectively.

This hands-on approach provides a solid foundation for designing advanced RAG-based applications in LangFlow.

Chapter 7: Enhancing Workflows with External Tools

Integrating external tools like APIs, plugins, and third-party services is a powerful way to extend the capabilities of LangFlow workflows. This chapter explores how to connect these resources, automate multi-modal applications, and implement a real-world example: building an image captioning system that generates text outputs.

7.1 APIs, Plugins, and Third-Party Integrations

What Are APIs, Plugins, and Third-Party Integrations?

- **APIs (Application Programming Interfaces)**: APIs allow workflows to interact with external systems and services, such as fetching live data or sending information to a database.

- **Plugins**: Extend the functionality of LangFlow by adding new capabilities or nodes to workflows.

- **Third-Party Integrations**: Tools or services outside LangFlow that can be connected, such as machine learning models, image processors, or payment gateways.

Why Use External Tools?

1. **Expand Capabilities**:

   o Incorporate features not natively available in LangFlow, such as live data retrieval or advanced analytics.

2. **Increase Efficiency**:

   o Automate repetitive tasks like data preprocessing or report generation.

3. **Enable Scalability**:

   o Leverage cloud-based APIs for high-performance computing or large-scale deployments.

Common Use Cases

Tool Type	Example	Use Case
API	OpenWeather API	Retrieve real-time weather data
Plugin	Sentiment Analysis Plugin	Analyze the sentiment of user input
Third-Party	Google Cloud Vision	Extract text from images

How to Integrate External Tools in LangFlow

1. **Identify the Tool**:

   o Choose an API, plugin, or third-party service relevant to your use case.

2. **Add a Node**:

   o In LangFlow, add a node representing the tool (e.g., an API call node or a custom plugin).

3. **Configure the Node**:

   o Enter required parameters like API keys, endpoints, or configurations.

4. **Connect to Workflow**:

   o Link the node to other parts of the workflow (e.g., input, LLM, or output nodes).

Code Example: Using an API in LangFlow

Objective:

Use OpenWeather API to fetch current weather data based on a user query.

python

```python
import requests

# Define the API endpoint and key
api_url = "http://api.openweathermap.org/data/2.5/weather"
api_key = "your_api_key"

# Function to fetch weather data
def get_weather(city):
    params = {"q": city, "appid": api_key, "units": "metric"}
    response = requests.get(api_url, params=params)
    if response.status_code == 200:
        data = response.json()
        return f"The weather in {city} is {data['weather'][0]['description']} at {data['main']['temp']}°C."
    else:
        return "Unable to fetch weather data."

# Example usage
print(get_weather("London"))
```

Key Considerations

- **Authentication**: Ensure you securely manage API keys and tokens.

- **Error Handling**: Implement fallback mechanisms in case the external tool is unavailable.

- **Rate Limits**: Be aware of API usage limits to avoid disruptions.

7.2 Automating Multi-Modal Applications

What Are Multi-Modal Applications?

Multi-modal applications process and integrate different types of data, such as:

- **Text**: User inputs, document processing.
- **Images**: Computer vision tasks like object detection.
- **Audio**: Speech-to-text and vice versa.

Why Automate Multi-Modal Applications?

1. **Improved User Experience**:
   - Combine multiple data sources for richer insights.

2. **Enhanced Functionality**:
   - Leverage AI to process diverse input types seamlessly.

3. **Efficiency**:
   - Automate tasks like transcription, image captioning, or data translation.

Steps to Build Multi-Modal Applications in LangFlow

1. **Input Configuration**:
   - Define nodes for each data type (e.g., text, image, audio).

2. **Processing**:
   - Add nodes for processing tasks, such as text summarization or image recognition.

3. **Output**:
   - Combine results into a unified format for presentation to the user.

Example: Text and Image Processing Workflow

Scenario:

Analyze an image for text (OCR) and summarize the extracted information.

1. **Input Node:**

   o Accepts the image from the user.

2. **Image Processing Node:**

   o Use an API like Google Cloud Vision for OCR.

3. **LLM Node:**

   o Summarize the extracted text.

4. **Output Node:**

   o Display the summarized information.

7.3 Real-World Example: Image Captioning with Text Output

Objective

Create a workflow that generates descriptive captions for images using an image recognition API and an LLM for text generation.

Steps to Build

Step 1: Define the Workflow

1. **Input:**

   o Accept an image from the user.

2. **Image Recognition:**

   o Use an API to identify objects or features in the image.

3. **Caption Generation:**

   o Generate a caption using an LLM.

4. **Output:**

- o Display the caption to the user.

Step 2: Configure LangFlow

1. Add the following nodes:

   - o **Input Node**: Upload the image.

   - o **API Node**: Connect to an image recognition service like Google Cloud Vision.

   - o **LLM Node**: Generate a caption based on the API's output.

   - o **Output Node**: Display the final caption.

Step 3: Example Implementation

Code Implementation:

python

```python
from google.cloud import vision
from langchain.llms import OpenAI

# Initialize Google Vision API client
client = vision.ImageAnnotatorClient()

# Function to analyze image
def analyze_image(image_path):
    with open(image_path, "rb") as image_file:
        content = image_file.read()
    image = vision.Image(content=content)
    response = client.label_detection(image=image)
    labels = [label.description for label in response.label_annotations]
    return labels

# Generate captions using LLM
llm = OpenAI(model_name="gpt-3.5-turbo", temperature=0.7)
def generate_caption(labels):
    prompt = f"Generate a descriptive caption for these objects: {', '.join(labels)}."
```

```
return llm.generate(prompt)

# Example usage
labels = analyze_image("example_image.jpg")
caption = generate_caption(labels)
print(caption)
```

Step 4: Test and Debug

1. **Input**: Upload an image of a beach scene.

2. **API Output**: Labels such as "beach," "sunset," "waves."

3. **LLM Output**: "A beautiful sunset over a serene beach with gentle waves."

Expected Outcome

By the end of this chapter, you will be able to:

1. Integrate APIs and plugins into LangFlow workflows.

2. Automate tasks in multi-modal applications.

3. Build and test an image captioning system using external tools.

LangFlow's flexibility and compatibility with external tools unlock limitless possibilities for enhancing workflows, ensuring you can meet a wide range of practical needs in AI development.

Chapter 8: Scaling and Optimizing Workflows

Optimizing and scaling LangFlow workflows is essential for building reliable, efficient, and scalable applications. This chapter provides in-depth guidance on token management, debugging workflows, leveraging analytics, and scaling solutions for both cloud and local environments.

8.1 Token Management and Efficiency
What Are Tokens in LLM Workflows?

Tokens are the building blocks of text processing in Large Language Models (LLMs). A token can be a word, part of a word, or even a punctuation mark.

- **Example**:

    o Sentence: "LangFlow simplifies workflows."

    o Tokens: ["Lang", "Flow", "simplifies", "work", "flows", "."]

Why Is Token Management Important?

1. **Cost Control**:

    o Many LLMs, like OpenAI GPT models, charge based on token usage.

2. **Performance Optimization**:

    o Large token usage can slow down responses and increase latency.

3. **Output Quality**:

    o Controlling token limits ensures concise and relevant responses.

Best Practices for Token Management

1. **Set Token Limits**:

    o Define maximum token usage for both input and output in your workflow.

2. **Optimize Prompts**:

    o Use clear, concise prompts to minimize unnecessary token consumption.

3. **Monitor Token Usage**:

    o Track token usage per query to identify inefficiencies.

Example: Configuring Token Limits in LangFlow

python

```
from langchain.llms import OpenAI

# Configure LLM with token limits
llm = OpenAI(model_name="gpt-3.5-turbo", max_tokens=100, temperature=0.7)

# Generate response
prompt = "Explain the benefits of LangFlow in a single paragraph."
response = llm.generate(prompt)
print(response)
```

Token Optimization Tips

Challenge	Solution
Overly verbose responses	Set stricter token limits and refine prompts.
High costs for frequent queries	Use summarization nodes to condense responses.
Inefficient data processing	Preprocess input data to remove redundant information.

8.2 Debugging and Workflow Analytics

Debugging Workflows

Debugging is essential for identifying and resolving issues in workflows. LangFlow provides tools and strategies for efficient debugging.

Common Debugging Challenges

Issue	Cause	Solution
Nodes not passing data	Incorrect input/output connections	Reconnect nodes correctly.
Unexpected outputs	Poorly configured prompts or tools	Refine prompts and validate node settings.
Workflow crashes	Missing data or misconfigured nodes	Test each node individually.

Steps for Debugging in LangFlow

1. **Monitor Node Logs**:

   o   LangFlow provides logs for each node. Review them to identify where errors occur.

2. **Validate Data Flow**:

   o   Use LangFlow's visual interface to trace the path of data between nodes.

3. **Use Test Inputs**:

   o   Test individual nodes with controlled inputs to isolate issues.

Example Debugging Workflow

Scenario: A chatbot workflow is returning irrelevant responses.

Steps:

1. **Check Input Node**:

o   Ensure the query is being captured correctly.

2. **Test Retrieval Node**:

   o   Verify that the knowledge base is returning relevant data.

3. **Refine LLM Node**:

   o   Adjust the prompt to improve context and accuracy.

Workflow Analytics

Analytics help monitor the performance and efficiency of workflows.

Metrics to Monitor

Metric	Description
Token Usage	Tracks the number of tokens used per query.
Latency	Measures the time taken for the workflow to execute.
Error Rate	Identifies the frequency of node or workflow failures.
Throughput	Measures the number of queries processed over time.

Tools for Analytics in LangFlow

1. **Built-in Monitoring**:

   o   LangFlow provides dashboards to track workflow performance.

2. **Third-Party Integrations**:

   o   Integrate with analytics tools like Grafana or Prometheus for advanced monitoring.

8.3 Scaling for Performance: Cloud and Local Options

Why Scale Workflows?

Scaling ensures that workflows can handle increased load and maintain performance as usage grows.

Scaling Options

1. **Local Scaling**:

   o Suitable for small-scale or prototype workflows.

   o Limited by local hardware resources.

2. **Cloud Scaling**:

   o Ideal for production-level workflows with high traffic.

   o Leverages cloud resources for scalability and reliability.

Steps to Scale Locally

1. **Optimize Resource Usage**:

   o Ensure workflows are efficient and avoid unnecessary computation.

2. **Leverage Parallel Processing**:

   o Run multiple workflows simultaneously to increase throughput.

3. **Use Hardware Acceleration**:

   o Utilize GPUs for tasks like vector search or model inference.

Example: Local Deployment

python

```
from langchain.vectorstores import FAISS
```

```
# Load vector store locally
vector_store = FAISS.load_local("knowledge_base_index")

# Query processing
query = "Explain renewable energy benefits."
results = vector_store.similarity_search(query, top_k=3)
print(results)
```

Steps to Scale in the Cloud

1. **Choose a Cloud Provider**:

   o   Options include AWS, Google Cloud, Azure.

2. **Deploy Scalable Infrastructure**:

   o   Use containers (e.g., Docker) or serverless functions for workflows.

3. **Leverage Cloud Databases and APIs**:

   o   Use managed vector stores like Pinecone or Weaviate.

Example: Cloud Deployment

Scenario: Deploying a chatbot with LangFlow on AWS.

1. **Containerize Workflow**:

   o   Package LangFlow and its dependencies in a Docker container.

2. **Deploy to AWS**:

   o   Use AWS ECS (Elastic Container Service) for scalability.

3. **Integrate Cloud Database**:

   o   Use DynamoDB or an S3 bucket for data storage.

Scaling Considerations

Factor	Local Scaling	Cloud Scaling
Cost	Lower upfront costs	Pay-as-you-go model
Flexibility	Limited by hardware	High flexibility with dynamic scaling
Complexity	Simpler setup	Requires cloud infrastructure expertise

Expected Outcome

By the end of this chapter, you will:

1. Understand how to manage tokens efficiently to reduce costs and improve performance.

2. Master debugging techniques and workflow analytics for robust applications.

3. Learn how to scale workflows locally and in the cloud for high performance.

Scaling and optimizing workflows in LangFlow ensures they remain efficient, reliable, and ready to handle real-world demands, making them an essential skill for every AI developer.

Chapter 9: Advanced RAG Applications

Retrieval-Augmented Generation (RAG) is a versatile approach for creating powerful AI systems, and its capabilities can be amplified when combined with multi-agent systems and optimized for enterprise applications. In this chapter, we explore advanced RAG concepts, focusing on integrating multi-agent systems, optimizing knowledge retrieval, and building an enterprise-grade question answering system.

9.1 Combining RAG with Multi-Agent Systems
What Are Multi-Agent Systems?

Multi-agent systems consist of multiple autonomous agents working together to accomplish tasks. In the context of RAG, agents can handle various roles:

1. **Data Retrieval Agent**: Fetches relevant knowledge from a database or vector store.

2. **Processing Agent**: Prepares and filters the retrieved data for downstream tasks.

3. **Generation Agent**: Uses an LLM to generate human-readable responses.

Benefits of Combining RAG with Multi-Agent Systems

1. **Task Specialization**:

   o Each agent performs a specific function, increasing efficiency.

2. **Scalability**:

   o Workflows can be expanded with additional agents for complex tasks.

3. **Flexibility**:

- Modular design allows agents to be reused or replaced.

Steps to Integrate Multi-Agent Systems with RAG

1. **Define Agent Roles**:

   - Assign tasks to each agent, such as retrieval, filtering, or generation.

2. **Design the Workflow**:

   - Use LangFlow to visually connect agents and establish data flow.

3. **Enable Communication**:

   - Set up data-sharing mechanisms between agents using nodes and edges.

Example: Multi-Agent RAG Workflow

Scenario:

Building a research assistant with specialized agents.

1. **Input**: A user enters a research query.

2. **Data Retrieval Agent**: Fetches relevant academic papers from a vector store.

3. **Processing Agent**: Filters the papers based on relevance and summarizes key points.

4. **Generation Agent**: Uses an LLM to create a concise research summary.

Implementation in LangFlow:

1. Add nodes for:

   - Input, retrieval, processing, and generation.

2. Connect the agents visually in LangFlow.

3. Configure each node with its specific task parameters.

9.2 Optimizing Knowledge Retrieval for Speed and Accuracy

Why Optimize Knowledge Retrieval?

1. **Improve Speed**:

   o   Faster retrieval ensures low-latency responses.

2. **Enhance Accuracy**:

   o   Accurate retrieval leads to more relevant and meaningful outputs.

Techniques for Optimizing Retrieval

1. **Preprocessing Data**:

   o   Chunk data into manageable pieces to improve retrieval accuracy.

   o   Use tools like NLTK or spaCy for text preprocessing.

2. **Use Advanced Vector Stores**:

   o   Tools like FAISS, Pinecone, or Weaviate allow for faster and more efficient vector searches.

3. **Adjust Query Embeddings**:

   o   Tailor query embeddings to better match the underlying data.

Best Practices

Optimization Technique	Impact
Chunk text into smaller passages	Improves precision during retrieval
Use dimensionality reduction	Speeds up vector searches
Fine-tune retrieval algorithms	Ensures that highly relevant results are ranked first

Code Example: Optimizing Retrieval

Objective:

Implement a retrieval system with optimized indexing and searching.
python

```python
from langchain.embeddings import OpenAIEmbeddings
from langchain.vectorstores import FAISS
from sklearn.decomposition import PCA

# Step 1: Generate embeddings for documents
documents = ["AI in healthcare", "AI in education", "AI in transportation"]
embedding_model = OpenAIEmbeddings()
document_embeddings = [embedding_model.embed(text) for text in documents]

# Step 2: Optimize embeddings using PCA
pca = PCA(n_components=50)
reduced_embeddings = pca.fit_transform(document_embeddings)

# Step 3: Index documents in FAISS
vector_store = FAISS.from_embeddings(reduced_embeddings, documents)

# Step 4: Perform a query
query_embedding = embedding_model.embed("AI applications in healthcare")
results = vector_store.similarity_search(query_embedding, top_k=3)
print(results)
```

9.3 Example: Enterprise-Grade Question Answering System
Objective

Develop an enterprise-level question answering (QA) system capable of handling diverse queries by combining RAG, multi-agent systems, and optimized knowledge retrieval.

Steps to Build

Step 1: Define Requirements

1. **Scalability**:

   o Handle high query volumes.

2. **Accuracy**:

   o Provide precise and contextually relevant answers.

3. **Speed**:

   o Ensure minimal response latency.

Step 2: Design the Workflow

1. **Input Node**:

   o Accepts user queries.

2. **Retriever Agent**:

   o Fetches relevant information from enterprise knowledge bases.

3. **Filter Agent**:

   o Filters data for relevance.

4. **LLM Agent**:

   o Generates a human-readable response.

5. **Output Node**:

   o Displays the response.

Step 3: Example Implementation

Code Example:

python

```
from langchain.llms import OpenAI
from langchain.vectorstores import FAISS
from langchain.prompts import PromptTemplate

# Step 1: Load vector store
```

```
vector_store = FAISS.load_local("enterprise_knowledge_base")

# Step 2: Define agents
retriever_agent = vector_store.similarity_search
filter_agent = lambda results: [result for result in results if "priority" in result]
llm_agent = OpenAI(model_name="gpt-3.5-turbo")

# Step 3: Build the QA pipeline
def enterprise_qa_pipeline(query):
    # Retrieve data
    retrieved_data = retriever_agent(query, top_k=5)
    # Filter data
    filtered_data = filter_agent(retrieved_data)
    # Generate response
    prompt = PromptTemplate(template="Based on the following data: {data},
answer the query: {query}")
    response = llm_agent.generate(prompt.format(data=filtered_data,
query=query))
    return response

# Step 4: Test the system
query = "What are our company's sustainability initiatives?"
response = enterprise_qa_pipeline(query)
print(response)
```

Testing and Optimization

1. **Test Query Variations**:

   o Use diverse user queries to validate retrieval accuracy and response quality.

2. **Optimize Agents**:

   o Adjust the filter agent's logic for relevance.

3. **Monitor System Performance**:

   o Use tools to measure latency, token usage, and accuracy.

Expected System Behavior

1. Query: "What is the company's carbon-neutral goal?"

    o **Retriever Agent**: Fetches sustainability reports and goals.

    o **Filter Agent**: Selects the section discussing carbon neutrality.

    o **LLM Agent**: Generates: "The company aims to achieve carbon neutrality by 2030."

Expected Outcome

By the end of this chapter, readers will:

1. Understand how to integrate RAG with multi-agent systems for advanced workflows.

2. Learn techniques for optimizing knowledge retrieval to balance speed and accuracy.

3. Build an enterprise-grade QA system using LangFlow, RAG, and multi-agent capabilities.

These advanced RAG applications unlock the potential for scalable, efficient, and accurate AI systems that can meet the demands of complex real-world use cases.

Chapter 10: Customizing LangFlow

Customizing LangFlow allows developers to adapt workflows to unique requirements by creating custom nodes, integrating Python code, and following best practices for modular workflow design. This chapter provides a detailed guide on building custom nodes and plugins, extending LangFlow's capabilities with Python, and designing modular workflows for scalability and reusability.

10.1 Creating Custom Nodes and Plugins

What Are Custom Nodes and Plugins?

- **Custom Nodes**: New building blocks in LangFlow workflows that handle specialized tasks not covered by default nodes.

- **Plugins**: Extensions that add new functionalities to LangFlow, such as external integrations or advanced processing capabilities.

Why Create Custom Nodes and Plugins?

1. **Expand Capabilities**:

   o Address specific needs not available in standard nodes.

2. **Streamline Workflows**:

   o Simplify complex tasks by encapsulating logic in reusable components.

3. **Integrate Proprietary Systems**:

   o Connect workflows to in-house tools or APIs.

Steps to Create a Custom Node

1. **Define the Node's Purpose**:

   o Determine the specific function your custom node will perform.

2. **Develop the Node Logic**:

   o Write the processing logic in Python or another supported language.

3. **Integrate the Node into LangFlow**:

   o Add the node to LangFlow's configuration so it appears in the interface.

Example: Creating a Sentiment Analysis Node

Objective:

Create a custom node that analyzes the sentiment of user input.

Implementation:

1. **Write the Node Logic**:

python

```python
from textblob import TextBlob

def analyze_sentiment(text):
    analysis = TextBlob(text)
    sentiment_score = analysis.sentiment.polarity
    return "Positive" if sentiment_score > 0 else "Negative" if sentiment_score < 0 else "Neutral"
```

2. **Register the Node in LangFlow**:

   o Add the following configuration to LangFlow:

json

```json
{
    "node_name": "Sentiment Analysis",
    "description": "Analyzes sentiment of user input",
    "input": ["text"],
    "output": ["sentiment"],
    "function": "analyze_sentiment"
```

}

3. **Connect the Node in a Workflow**:

   o Use the node to process user queries and pass the
     sentiment result to the next node.

Testing Custom Nodes

- Test the node independently with sample inputs to validate
  its logic.

- Integrate it into workflows and check for compatibility with
  other nodes.

10.2 Extending LangFlow with Python

LangFlow supports Python as a scripting language, allowing users
to add advanced logic and extend functionality.

Why Use Python?

1. **Flexibility**:

   o Python enables custom data processing, API calls, and
     advanced algorithms.

2. **Rich Libraries**:

   o Leverage Python's extensive library ecosystem for
     tasks like machine learning, natural language
     processing, and data visualization.

3. **Ease of Integration**:

   o LangFlow workflows can easily execute Python
     scripts.

Steps to Extend LangFlow with Python

1. **Identify the Requirement**:

- o Determine the specific functionality to be added using Python.

2. **Write the Python Script**:

   - o Develop the logic to handle the task.

3. **Integrate the Script in LangFlow**:

   - o Use LangFlow's scripting nodes to execute the Python code.

Example: Adding a Summarization Function

Objective:

Extend LangFlow to summarize large text inputs using Python.

Implementation:

1. **Write the Summarization Script**:

python

```
from transformers import pipeline

# Load summarization pipeline
summarizer = pipeline("summarization")

def summarize_text(text):
    summary = summarizer(text, max_length=50, min_length=25,
do_sample=False)
    return summary[0]['summary_text']
```

2. **Integrate the Script**:

   - o Add the script to a LangFlow node using the scripting interface.

3. **Connect in a Workflow**:

   - o Use the summarization node to process long user inputs and pass the result to the LLM node.

4. **Test the Workflow**:

- Input: "LangFlow is a visual interface for building AI workflows..."

- Output: "LangFlow simplifies AI workflow creation with its visual tools."

10.3 Best Practices for Modular Workflow Design
What Is Modular Workflow Design?

Modular design involves creating workflows as a collection of independent, reusable components (nodes). This approach enhances scalability, flexibility, and maintainability.

Key Principles

1. **Reusability**:

   - Design nodes that can be reused across multiple workflows.

2. **Encapsulation**:

   - Keep each node focused on a single task to simplify debugging and updates.

3. **Interoperability**:

   - Ensure nodes work seamlessly with other components.

Advantages

1. **Simplified Maintenance**:

   - Changes to one node don't disrupt the entire workflow.

2. **Scalability**:

   - Modular workflows are easier to scale by adding new components.

3. **Faster Development**:

- o Reusable nodes accelerate the creation of new workflows.

Steps to Create Modular Workflows

1. **Identify Common Tasks**:

   - o Break down workflows into smaller, reusable tasks.

2. **Standardize Node Inputs/Outputs**:

   - o Define clear input and output formats for each node.

3. **Test Independently**:

   - o Validate nodes in isolation before integrating them.

Example: Modular Workflow for Customer Support

Workflow Design:

1. **Input Node**:

   - o Captures user queries.

2. **Sentiment Analysis Node**:

   - o Determines the sentiment of the query.

3. **Retrieval Node**:

   - o Fetches relevant FAQs based on the query.

4. **Response Generation Node**:

   - o Generates a response using an LLM.

Testing and Refining Modular Workflows

1. Test each node with varied inputs to ensure robustness.

2. Use workflow analytics to identify bottlenecks and optimize performance.

Best Practices Summary

Practice	Benefit
Encapsulate logic in nodes	Simplifies updates and debugging
Use clear naming conventions	Improves workflow readability and maintenance
Document workflows	Ensures team collaboration and future reuse
Optimize node connections	Reduces data flow latency and improves performance

Expected Outcomes

By the end of this chapter, you will:

1. Understand how to create and integrate custom nodes and plugins.

2. Extend LangFlow's functionality with Python for advanced use cases.

3. Design modular workflows that are scalable, maintainable, and efficient.

Customizing LangFlow unlocks its full potential, empowering developers to create tailored workflows that address unique challenges and drive innovation in AI applications.

Chapter 11: Case Study: Customer Support Automation

Customer support is one of the most impactful applications of AI workflows. Automating responses to Frequently Asked Questions (FAQs) and integrating with external Customer Relationship Management (CRM) systems and knowledge bases can greatly improve efficiency, reduce operational costs, and enhance customer satisfaction. This chapter presents a detailed case study on designing and implementing a LangFlow workflow for customer support automation.

11.1 Designing a Workflow for Dynamic FAQs

Dynamic FAQ workflows allow AI to respond intelligently to customer queries by retrieving relevant information and generating tailored responses.

Key Features of a Dynamic FAQ Workflow

1. **Real-Time Query Handling**:
    o Respond to customer inquiries instantly.

2. **Contextual Understanding**:
    o Interpret the intent behind customer queries.

3. **Knowledge Retrieval**:
    o Fetch the most relevant answers from a knowledge base.

4. **Response Generation**:
    o Use an LLM to deliver a natural-sounding reply.

Steps to Design a Dynamic FAQ Workflow

1. **Define Objectives**:
    o Provide accurate and timely answers to FAQs.

   o Handle a wide variety of customer queries effectively.

2. **Identify Components**:

   o Input node for customer queries.

   o Retrieval node for searching knowledge bases.

   o LLM node for generating responses.

   o Output node to display the responses.

3. **Set Up Knowledge Base**:

   o Use a vector store to store FAQ data for efficient retrieval.

4. **Integrate and Test**:

   o Combine the nodes into a cohesive workflow and test with sample queries.

Example Workflow Design

Workflow Structure

1. **Input Node**: Captures customer queries.

2. **Retrieval Node**: Searches an FAQ database or vector store.

3. **LLM Node**: Processes the retrieved data and generates a response.

4. **Output Node**: Displays the response to the customer.

Implementation Example

Code Implementation:

python

```python
from langchain.llms import OpenAI
from langchain.vectorstores import FAISS
from langchain.prompts import PromptTemplate
```

```
# Step 1: Load the FAQ knowledge base
vector_store = FAISS.load_local("faq_knowledge_base")

# Step 2: Configure the LLM
llm = OpenAI(model_name="gpt-3.5-turbo", temperature=0.7)

# Step 3: Define the FAQ retrieval function
def get_faq_response(query):
    # Retrieve relevant documents
    retrieved_docs = vector_store.similarity_search(query, top_k=3)

    # Combine retrieved content
    combined_content = " ".join([doc for doc in retrieved_docs])

    # Generate a response using LLM
    prompt = PromptTemplate(template="Based on the following FAQs:
{content}, answer the query: {query}")
    response = llm.generate(prompt.format(content=combined_content,
query=query))
    return response

# Example Query
query = "How do I reset my password?"
response = get_faq_response(query)
print(response)
```

Testing the Workflow

- **Input**: "What is your return policy?"

- **Expected Output**: "Our return policy allows returns within 30 days of purchase with a receipt."

11.2 Integrating with External CRMs and Knowledge Bases

Why Integrate with CRMs and Knowledge Bases?

1. **Centralized Information**:
   - CRMs store customer details, enabling personalized interactions.
2. **Enhanced Data Access**:
   - Knowledge bases provide a repository for FAQs, product documentation, and policies.
3. **Improved Automation**:
   - Seamlessly fetch and update information across systems.

Steps to Integrate with External CRMs

1. **Choose a CRM**:
   - Popular options include Salesforce, HubSpot, and Zoho CRM.
2. **Set Up API Access**:
   - Use the CRM's API to retrieve or update customer data.
3. **Connect CRM to LangFlow**:
   - Add a custom node in LangFlow to handle CRM interactions.

Example: Integrating Salesforce with LangFlow

Objective:

Fetch customer data from Salesforce and personalize responses.

Implementation:

python

```python
import requests

# Step 1: Authenticate with Salesforce API
def authenticate_salesforce():
    url = "https://your_salesforce_instance.salesforce.com/services/oauth2/token"
    payload = {
        "grant_type": "password",
        "client_id": "your_client_id",
        "client_secret": "your_client_secret",
        "username": "your_username",
        "password": "your_password"
    }
    response = requests.post(url, data=payload)
    return response.json()["access_token"]

# Step 2: Retrieve Customer Data
def get_customer_data(customer_id, access_token):
    headers = {"Authorization": f"Bearer {access_token}"}
    url = f"https://your_salesforce_instance.salesforce.com/services/data/v52.0/sobjects/Contact/{customer_id}"
    response = requests.get(url, headers=headers)
    return response.json()

# Step 3: Example Integration
access_token = authenticate_salesforce()
customer_data = get_customer_data("0031g000008cXZfAAO", access_token)
print(customer_data)
```

Steps to Integrate with Knowledge Bases

1. **Select a Knowledge Base**:
   - Use vector stores like FAISS, Pinecone, or Weaviate.
2. **Index the Data**:

o Preprocess and store FAQs, documents, or articles in the vector store.

3. **Enable Querying**:

   o Use similarity search to retrieve relevant content.

Real-World Example: Combining CRM and Knowledge Base Integration

Objective:

Create a customer support workflow that:

1. Personalizes responses using CRM data.

2. Retrieves answers from the knowledge base.

Workflow Design

1. **Input Node**:

   o Accepts customer queries and IDs.

2. **CRM Node**:

   o Retrieves customer details from the CRM.

3. **Retrieval Node**:

   o Searches the FAQ knowledge base.

4. **LLM Node**:

   o Combines CRM data and FAQ content to generate a personalized response.

5. **Output Node**:

   o Displays the response to the customer.

Implementation Example

python

```python
def personalized_response(query, customer_id):
    # Retrieve customer details
    customer_data = get_customer_data(customer_id, access_token)
    customer_name = customer_data.get("Name", "Customer")

    # Retrieve FAQ content
    faq_response = get_faq_response(query)

    # Personalize the response
    return f"Hi {customer_name}, here's the information you requested:
{faq_response}"
```

Benefits of Integration

Benefit	Description
Personalization	Tailor responses based on customer history or preferences.
Efficiency	Automate repetitive support tasks with real-time data.
Scalability	Handle large volumes of queries without manual intervention.

Expected Outcomes

By the end of this chapter, you will:

1. Design a dynamic FAQ workflow for automated customer support.

2. Learn how to integrate LangFlow with CRMs and knowledge bases.

3. Build a personalized, efficient, and scalable customer support solution.

This comprehensive approach demonstrates how LangFlow can revolutionize customer support by combining intelligent automation with seamless integrations.

Chapter 12: Case Study: Research Assistant with RAG

Research assistants play a vital role in academia, where automation can significantly enhance the speed and accuracy of literature reviews and data synthesis. This chapter explores how Retrieval-Augmented Generation (RAG) can automate academic workflows, providing a practical guide for building a research assistant. We will cover the end-to-end process, from query to actionable insights, and discuss its real-world applications in academic research.

12.1 Automating Literature Review
What is a Literature Review?

A literature review involves analyzing, synthesizing, and summarizing academic papers, articles, and research findings to provide insights into a specific topic. Automating this process can:

1. **Save Time**: Quickly gather and summarize large volumes of data.

2. **Enhance Accuracy**: Minimize human error during data retrieval and synthesis.

3. **Promote Discovery**: Identify patterns or insights often missed in manual reviews.

Steps to Automate a Literature Review with RAG

Step 1: Define Objectives

- **Primary Goal**: Retrieve relevant academic papers and generate summaries or actionable insights.

- **Secondary Goals**: Organize retrieved data, identify key themes, and generate concise overviews.

Step 2: Build the Workflow

Workflow Structure:

1. **Input Node**:
   - Accepts user queries, such as "Recent advancements in AI ethics."

2. **Retrieval Node**:
   - Searches a vector store containing indexed academic papers.

3. **LLM Node**:
   - Synthesizes retrieved information into a coherent summary.

4. **Output Node**:
   - Presents the summary and optionally stores insights in a database.

Step 3: Index the Literature

1. **Preprocess Academic Papers**:
   - Chunk long documents into manageable segments.
   - Example: Split a research paper into sections like Introduction, Methods, and Results.

2. **Generate Embeddings**:
   - Use a pre-trained model to convert text into vector representations for similarity searches.

Code Example:

python

```
from langchain.embeddings import OpenAIEmbeddings
from langchain.vectorstores import FAISS
```

```
# Sample academic data
documents = [
    "AI ethics focuses on fairness and accountability.",
    "Deep learning advancements include transformer models.",
    "AI in healthcare improves diagnostics and treatment."
]

# Generate embeddings
embedding_model = OpenAIEmbeddings()
document_embeddings = [embedding_model.embed(text) for text in documents]

# Create a vector store
vector_store = FAISS.from_embeddings(document_embeddings, documents)

# Save the vector store
vector_store.save_local("academic_index")
```

3. **Load Vector Store**:
   o Make the indexed data available for querying.

python

```
vector_store = FAISS.load_local("academic_index")
```

Step 4: Query the Knowledge Base

Retrieve the most relevant academic texts using a similarity search.

\

Code Example:

python

```
query = "Explain transformer advancements in AI."
results = vector_store.similarity_search(query, top_k=3)
print(results)
```

Step 5: Synthesize Insights

Use an LLM to generate a summary from the retrieved data.

Code Example:

python

```
from langchain.llms import OpenAI

# Initialize LLM
llm = OpenAI(model_name="gpt-3.5-turbo", temperature=0.5)

# Generate summary
def generate_summary(query, retrieved_docs):
    combined_text = " ".join(retrieved_docs)
    prompt = f"Summarize the following documents in relation to the query:
{query}\n{combined_text}"
    return llm.generate(prompt)

summary = generate_summary(query, results)
print(summary)
```

Testing the Literature Review Workflow

Test Input: "Discuss AI's role in personalized medicine."

- **Retrieval Node**: Fetches relevant papers on AI in healthcare.

- **LLM Node Output**: "AI in personalized medicine enables tailored treatment by analyzing patient-specific data using predictive models."

12.2 Real-World Application in Academic Research
The Role of RAG in Academia

RAG-based research assistants are transforming academic research by:

1. **Accelerating Discovery**:

   o   Researchers can review large datasets quickly, enabling faster breakthroughs.

2. **Improving Collaboration**:

   o   Automated tools can provide summaries or highlights for teams working on multi-disciplinary research.

3. **Enhancing Accessibility**:

   o   Simplify complex topics for broader audiences, including students and policymakers.

Use Cases

1. Literature Reviews for Grant Proposals

- **Problem**: Researchers need to justify their proposals with evidence from recent studies.

- **Solution**: A research assistant retrieves and summarizes relevant publications, highlighting trends and gaps in the field.

2. Academic Writing Support

- **Problem**: Writing papers or reviews requires extensive synthesis of existing work.

- **Solution**: A RAG assistant generates drafts based on selected sources, saving time and effort.

Example Workflow: Literature Review for AI in Education

Objective:

Analyze the impact of AI on education and summarize key findings.

Workflow Steps:

1. **Input Node:**

     o Query: "What are the benefits of AI in education?"

2. **Retrieval Node:**

     o Searches a vector store with indexed academic papers on education and AI.

3. **Processing Node:**

     o Filters results for relevance and synthesizes summaries.

4. **LLM Node:**

     o Generates a concise, well-structured summary.

5. **Output Node:**

     o Displays the summary and stores it in a report format.

Code Implementation:

python

```python
def research_workflow(query):
    # Retrieve relevant documents
    retrieved_docs = vector_store.similarity_search(query, top_k=5)

    # Combine documents
    combined_text = " ".join(retrieved_docs)

    # Generate a response
```

```
    prompt = f"Summarize the following documents for the query:
{query}\n{combined_text}"
    response = llm.generate(prompt)
    return response

# Test the workflow
query = "Impact of AI in education."
response = research_workflow(query)
print(response)
```

Challenges and Solutions

Challenge	Solution
Data Overload	Use chunking and relevance filters to manage large datasets.
Inconsistent Data Quality	Preprocess and curate data before indexing.
Complex Query Requirements	Leverage advanced prompts to tailor retrieval and generation.

Expected Outcomes

By the end of this chapter, you will:

1. Understand how to automate literature reviews using RAG workflows.

2. Learn how to set up and query vector stores for academic data.

3. Build and test a research assistant capable of synthesizing insights from complex datasets.

This case study highlights the potential of RAG to revolutionize academic workflows, making research faster, more accurate, and highly accessible.

Chapter 13: Case Study: Data-Driven Decision Pipelines

In the modern business landscape, data-driven decision-making is crucial for maintaining a competitive edge. Automating the retrieval, processing, and analysis of data ensures efficiency, accuracy, and actionable insights. This chapter explores how LangFlow can powerfully combine Retrieval-Augmented Generation (RAG) and workflow automation to create data-driven decision pipelines for business intelligence.

13.1 Automating Data Retrieval and Processing
The Importance of Data Retrieval and Processing

Businesses rely on timely and accurate data to make informed decisions. Automating these tasks reduces manual effort, eliminates errors, and accelerates workflows.

Key Features of Automated Data Pipelines

1. **Real-Time Data Retrieval**:

    o   Fetch updated information from APIs, databases, or internal systems.

2. **Data Cleaning and Transformation**:

    o   Ensure data is in a usable format before analysis.

3. **Actionable Insights**:

    o   Use processed data to generate reports or trigger downstream actions.

Steps to Build a Data Retrieval and Processing Pipeline

Step 1: Define Objectives

- Retrieve specific datasets from external or internal sources.

- Process the data for analysis or direct decision-making.

Step 2: Workflow Design

Workflow Structure:

1. **Input Node**: Accepts parameters for data retrieval (e.g., date range, metrics).

2. **Retrieval Node**: Fetches data from APIs or databases.

3. **Processing Node**: Cleans and transforms the data.

4. **LLM Node**: Summarizes or interprets the data for business insights.

5. **Output Node**: Displays results in a report or sends alerts.

Step 3: Implementation

Code Example: Automating API Data Retrieval

python

```
import requests
import pandas as pd

# Step 1: Retrieve Data from API
def fetch_data(api_url, params):
    response = requests.get(api_url, params=params)
    if response.status_code == 200:
        return response.json()
    else:
        raise Exception("API call failed with status code:", response.status_code)

# Step 2: Process and Clean Data
def process_data(raw_data):
    # Convert JSON to DataFrame
    df = pd.DataFrame(raw_data)
    # Perform cleaning
```

```
df = df.dropna()  # Remove null values
    df['date'] = pd.to_datetime(df['date'])  # Convert date strings to datetime
objects
    return df

# Step 3: Example Usage
api_url = "https://api.example.com/sales"
params = {"start_date": "2023-01-01", "end_date": "2023-01-31"}
raw_data = fetch_data(api_url, params)
cleaned_data = process_data(raw_data)

print(cleaned_data.head())
```

Testing the Pipeline

Input: Retrieve sales data for January 2023.

- **Expected Output**: A cleaned DataFrame with columns like date, product, and sales_amount.

Benefits of Automation

1. **Speed**:

    o Retrieve and process large datasets in seconds.

2. **Scalability**:

    o Handle multiple data sources simultaneously.

3. **Accuracy**:

    o Eliminate manual errors through consistent automation.

13.2 Workflow Optimization for Business Intelligence
What is Business Intelligence (BI)?

Business Intelligence involves using data analysis tools and techniques to transform raw data into actionable insights. BI pipelines often include data retrieval, transformation, visualization, and reporting.

Optimizing Data Pipelines for BI

Key Considerations for Optimization

1. **Data Retrieval Speed**:

   o Use caching or parallel requests for faster access.

2. **Scalability**:

   o Design workflows to handle growing data volumes.

3. **Integration**:

   o Connect workflows with BI tools like Tableau or Power BI for visualization.

Steps to Optimize BI Workflows

1. **Parallelize Data Retrieval**:

   o Fetch data from multiple sources concurrently.

2. **Implement Data Validation**:

   o Verify data integrity during processing.

3. **Leverage LLMs for Analysis**:

   o Use language models to summarize trends, identify anomalies, or predict outcomes.

Real-World Example: Sales Performance Dashboard

Objective:

Automate the creation of a sales performance dashboard using LangFlow.

Workflow Design

1. **Input Node**:

   o Accepts parameters like date range or region.

2. **Data Retrieval Node**:

   o Fetches sales data from an API.

3. **Processing Node**:

   o Cleans, aggregates, and transforms data for visualization.

4. **Analysis Node**:

   o Uses an LLM to summarize trends or flag anomalies.

5. **Output Node**:

   o Exports results to a BI tool or generates a report.

Code Implementation

python

```python
from langchain.llms import OpenAI
import pandas as pd

# Step 1: Fetch and Process Data
def fetch_and_process(api_url, params):
    response = requests.get(api_url, params=params)
    raw_data = response.json()
    df = pd.DataFrame(raw_data)
    df['date'] = pd.to_datetime(df['date'])
    return df.groupby('region')['sales'].sum()

# Step 2: Summarize Data with LLM
```

```python
def generate_summary(data):
    llm = OpenAI(model_name="gpt-3.5-turbo")
    prompt = f"Summarize the sales performance for the following data:
{data.to_dict()}"
    return llm.generate(prompt)

# Step 3: Example Workflow
api_url = "https://api.example.com/sales"
params = {"start_date": "2023-01-01", "end_date": "2023-01-31"}
sales_data = fetch_and_process(api_url, params)
summary = generate_summary(sales_data)

print("Sales Summary:")
print(summary)
```

Testing and Refinement

1. **Input**: Parameters for sales data retrieval.

2. **Output**: A summary like:

   o   "Region A achieved the highest sales with $50,000, while Region B reported a decline."

Challenges and Solutions

Challenge	Solution
Slow API Responses	Implement caching or batch retrieval.
Data Quality Issues	Add data validation and error handling during processing.
Complex Analysis	Leverage LLMs for advanced data

Challenge	Solution
Needs	interpretation and predictions.

Integrating LangFlow with BI Tools

To enhance visualization and reporting, connect LangFlow workflows with tools like Tableau, Power BI, or Google Data Studio.

Steps:

1. **Export Data**:

   o Use CSV, JSON, or direct database connections for seamless integration.

2. **Automate Updates**:

   o Schedule workflows to retrieve and process data regularly.

3. **Visualize Insights**:

   o Create dashboards showcasing trends, KPIs, and alerts.

Expected Outcomes

By the end of this chapter, you will:

1. Build an automated pipeline for data retrieval and processing.

2. Optimize workflows for business intelligence applications.

3. Integrate LangFlow workflows with BI tools for actionable insights.

Data-driven decision pipelines powered by LangFlow enable businesses to automate routine tasks, gain deeper insights, and make informed decisions faster, setting the foundation for smarter, more efficient operations.

Chapter 14: Case Study: Multi-Modal Applications

Multi-modal applications leverage multiple types of data—such as text, images, and APIs—to create powerful workflows. These workflows enable solutions like personalized product recommendations, real-time sentiment analysis, and enhanced customer engagement. In this chapter, we explore integrating diverse data types and building a real-world application for product recommendations.

14.1 Integrating Text, Images, and APIs
What Are Multi-Modal Applications?

Multi-modal applications combine different data modalities—text, images, audio, and structured data—for a unified, comprehensive output. Examples include:

1. **Text and Images**: Summarizing articles with relevant images.

2. **Text and APIs**: Retrieving live data and generating explanations.

3. **Images and APIs**: Using image recognition to query external databases.

Why Use Multi-Modal Applications?

- **Enhanced User Experience**:

    o   Deliver richer, more interactive outputs.

- **Improved Decision-Making**:

    o   Use diverse data for more informed insights.

- **Scalability**:

o   Multi-modal workflows can adapt to various use
    cases.

Steps to Integrate Text, Images, and APIs

Step 1: Define the Workflow

- Combine multiple inputs (e.g., user query, uploaded image).

- Process each modality independently or in tandem.

- Merge results to generate unified insights.

Step 2: Design a Multi-Modal Pipeline

Workflow Structure:

1. **Input Nodes**:

   o   Text: Accept user queries or commands.

   o   Images: Allow users to upload images.

2. **Processing Nodes**:

   o   Text: Summarize, retrieve, or analyze input text.

   o   Images: Perform image recognition or categorization.

3. **API Nodes**:

   o   Fetch additional data (e.g., product details or weather
       information).

4. **LLM Node**:

   o   Combine results into a natural-language response.

5. **Output Node**:

   o   Display results in a user-friendly format.

Step 3: Implementation

Code Example: Multi-Modal Workflow for Product Categorization

python

```python
from PIL import Image
from transformers import pipeline
import requests

# Step 1: Image Recognition
def recognize_image(image_path):
    # Load image classification model
    image_classifier = pipeline("image-classification")
    return image_classifier(image_path)

# Step 2: Text Processing
def process_text(query):
    if "recommendations" in query.lower():
        return "Searching for product recommendations..."
    else:
        return "Unsupported query type."

# Step 3: API Integration
def fetch_product_details(category):
    api_url = f"https://api.example.com/products?category={category}"
    response = requests.get(api_url)
    if response.status_code == 200:
        return response.json()
    else:
        return {"error": "Unable to fetch data"}

# Step 4: Combine Results
def generate_response(image_path, query):
    # Recognize image
    image_result = recognize_image(image_path)
```

```python
category = image_result[0]["label"]

# Process query
text_result = process_text(query)

# Fetch product details
product_details = fetch_product_details(category)

# Generate final response
return {
    "query_analysis": text_result,
    "image_category": category,
    "product_recommendations": product_details
}

# Example Usage
response = generate_response("example_image.jpg", "Show me
recommendations")
print(response)
```

Testing the Pipeline

Input:

- Image: A photo of a chair.

- Query: "Show me recommendations."

Output:

json

```json
{
  "query_analysis": "Searching for product recommendations...",
  "image_category": "furniture",
  "product_recommendations": [
    {"name": "Ergonomic Chair", "price": "$199", "rating": "4.5"},
    {"name": "Office Chair", "price": "$149", "rating": "4.0"}
```

```
      ]
      }
```

Challenges and Solutions

Challenge	Solution
Inconsistent input formats	Standardize inputs during preprocessing.
High latency for API calls	Implement caching or parallel requests.
Difficulty in combining outputs	Use an LLM to integrate results coherently.

14.2 Real-World Example: Product Recommendations
Objective

Build a multi-modal application that recommends products based on user-uploaded images and queries.

Workflow Design

1. Inputs

- **Text Input**:

    - User query specifying their preferences (e.g., "recommend modern chairs").

- **Image Input**:

    - Uploaded photo of a desired product or style.

2. Processing

- **Image Processing**:

- Categorize the uploaded image (e.g., furniture, electronics).

- **Query Analysis**:
  - Extract user intent and preferences from text input.

- **Data Retrieval**:
  - Use APIs to fetch product recommendations based on category and preferences.

3. Output

- Display a list of personalized product recommendations with details such as:
  - Name
  - Price
  - Ratings
  - Purchase link

Code Implementation

python

```
from langchain.llms import OpenAI
from PIL import Image
import requests

# Image Recognition
def recognize_image(image_path):
    # Use an image recognition API
    api_url = "https://api.imagerecognition.com/classify"
    with open(image_path, "rb") as img:
```

```python
        response = requests.post(api_url, files={"file": img})
    return response.json()["category"]

# Query Processing
def analyze_query(query):
    return f"Analyzing query: {query}"

# Fetch Recommendations
def fetch_recommendations(category):
    api_url = f"https://api.example.com/recommendations?category={category}"
    response = requests.get(api_url)
    if response.status_code == 200:
        return response.json()["products"]
    else:
        return [{"error": "No recommendations available"}]

# Combine Results
def product_recommendation_workflow(image_path, query):
    category = recognize_image(image_path)
    query_analysis = analyze_query(query)
    recommendations = fetch_recommendations(category)
    return {
        "query_analysis": query_analysis,
        "category": category,
        "recommendations": recommendations
    }

# Example Usage
workflow_output = product_recommendation_workflow("chair_image.jpg", "I
need office furniture")
print(workflow_output)
```

Expected Output

json

```
{
  "query_analysis": "Analyzing query: I need office furniture",
  "category": "furniture",
  "recommendations": [
    {"name": "Ergonomic Desk Chair", "price": "$199", "rating": "4.7"},
    {"name": "Luxury Leather Chair", "price": "$299", "rating": "4.8"}
  ]
}
```

Benefits of Multi-Modal Applications for Product Recommendations

1. **Improved Personalization**:

   o Tailor recommendations based on user preferences and visual inputs.

2. **Enhanced Engagement**:

   o Interactive workflows improve user experience.

3. **Seamless Integration**:

   o Combine image recognition, text processing, and APIs effortlessly.

Challenges in Real-World Applications

Challenge	Solution
Incomplete or ambiguous inputs	Use fallback mechanisms or prompt users for additional details.
Scalability for high API traffic	Optimize API usage with batching and rate-limiting strategies.
Ensuring data security and privacy	Encrypt sensitive user data during storage and transfer.

Expected Outcomes

By the end of this chapter, you will:

1. Understand how to integrate text, images, and APIs in a unified workflow.

2. Build and test a product recommendation system using multi-modal data.

3. Learn best practices for handling challenges in real-world multi-modal applications.

Multi-modal workflows open doors to advanced applications across industries, from personalized shopping experiences to smarter content curation, making them an essential tool in the AI developer's arsenal.

Chapter 15: Deploying LangFlow Applications

Effective deployment is a crucial step in turning LangFlow workflows into operational AI applications. Whether deploying locally, in the cloud, or using a hybrid approach, ensuring scalability, reliability, and proper monitoring is key. This chapter provides an in-depth guide to deployment options and best practices for monitoring and logging deployed workflows.

15.1 Deployment Options: Local, Cloud, and Hybrid

Why Deployment Matters

Deployment transforms LangFlow workflows from development-stage prototypes into fully operational systems. The deployment method impacts scalability, cost, and accessibility.

Local Deployment

Definition: Workflows are deployed on local machines or private servers.

Advantages

1. **Full Control**:
   - Complete access to hardware and configurations.

2. **Data Security**:
   - Sensitive data remains on-premises.

3. **Cost-Effective**:
   - No recurring cloud service charges.

Challenges

1. **Limited Scalability**:

    o Dependent on local hardware capabilities.

2. **Maintenance Overhead**:

    o Requires manual updates and troubleshooting.

Steps for Local Deployment

1. **Prepare the Environment**:

    o Install dependencies using pip install langflow.

2. **Run the Workflow**:

bash

```
langflow --run <workflow_name>
```

3. **Test Locally**:

    o Validate inputs, outputs, and system performance.

Code Example:

bash

```
langflow --workflow-file my_workflow.json
```

Use Case:

*   Ideal for small-scale workflows or offline environments (e.g., secure enterprise applications).

Cloud Deployment

Definition: Workflows are hosted on cloud platforms like AWS, Google Cloud, or Azure.

\

Advantages

1. **Scalability**:
   - o Dynamically allocate resources based on workload.

2. **Global Accessibility**:
   - o Access workflows from anywhere.

3. **Integration**:
   - o Seamless connection with cloud APIs and databases.

Challenges

1. **Cost**:
   - o Usage-based pricing can add up.

2. **Data Privacy**:
   - o Requires secure handling of sensitive information.

Steps for Cloud Deployment

1. **Containerize the Workflow**:
   - o Use Docker to package the LangFlow application.

dockerfile

```
FROM python:3.9
WORKDIR /app
COPY . .
RUN pip install langflow
CMD ["langflow", "--workflow-file", "my_workflow.json"]
```

2. **Deploy to Cloud Platform**:
   - o Use services like AWS ECS or Google Kubernetes Engine (GKE).

3. **Configure Autoscaling**:
   - o Set up auto-scaling rules to manage high traffic.

Example Deployment:

bash

```
docker build -t langflow-app .
docker run -p 8080:8080 langflow-app
```

Use Case:

- Ideal for applications with high traffic or workflows requiring global access (e.g., customer support systems).

Hybrid Deployment

Definition: Combines local and cloud infrastructure, often to balance cost and performance.

Advantages

1. **Flexibility**:

    o Use cloud resources for heavy workloads while keeping sensitive tasks local.

2. **Cost Optimization**:

    o Pay for cloud services only when necessary.

Challenges

1. **Complexity**:

    o Requires seamless integration between local and cloud components.

2. **Latency**:

    o Communication delays between local and cloud systems.

Steps for Hybrid Deployment

1. **Identify Workload Distribution**:

o   Decide which tasks will run locally versus in the cloud.

2. **Set Up Secure Communication**:

   o   Use VPNs or encrypted APIs to connect local and cloud systems.

3. **Monitor Both Environments**:

   o   Ensure visibility into local and cloud operations.

Example:

- Local: Preprocess sensitive data.

- Cloud: Run computationally intensive tasks.

Comparison of Deployment Options

Feature	Local	Cloud	Hybrid
Scalability	Limited	High	Moderate
Cost	One-time	Usage-based	Balanced
Data Security	High	Requires encryption	Flexible based on workload
Accessibility	Limited	Global	Flexible

15.2 Monitoring and Logging for Deployed Workflows

Why Monitoring and Logging Matter

- **Performance Tracking**:

  o   Monitor latency, throughput, and resource usage.

- **Error Debugging**:

  o   Identify and resolve workflow issues.

- **Data Auditing**:

o   Track input/output for compliance and debugging.

Setting Up Monitoring

Metrics to Monitor

Metric	Description
Latency	Time taken for workflows to process requests.
Throughput	Number of requests handled per second.
Error Rate	Percentage of failed workflow executions.
Resource Usage	CPU, memory, and storage utilization.

Tools for Monitoring

1. **Built-in Monitoring**:

   o   LangFlow provides logs and basic monitoring capabilities.

2. **Third-Party Tools**:

   o   Use tools like Prometheus, Grafana, or CloudWatch for advanced monitoring.

Implementing Logging

Best Practices for Logging

1. **Log Levels**:

   o   Use levels like DEBUG, INFO, WARNING, ERROR, and CRITICAL.

2. **Structured Logs**:

   o   Store logs in a structured format (e.g., JSON) for easy parsing.

3. **Centralized Storage**:

- o Use cloud storage or logging platforms like ELK Stack.

Code Example: Logging in Python

python

```
import logging

# Configure logging
logging.basicConfig(
    filename="workflow.log",
    level=logging.INFO,
    format="%(asctime)s - %(levelname)s - %(message)s"
)

# Log workflow events
logging.info("Workflow started")
try:
    # Simulate workflow execution
    result = run_workflow("my_workflow.json")
    logging.info("Workflow completed successfully")
except Exception as e:
    logging.error(f"Workflow failed: {e}")
```

Integrating Monitoring and Logging in LangFlow

1. **Enable Workflow Logs**:

    - o Configure LangFlow to log events during workflow execution.

2. **Set Up Dashboards**:

    - o Use Grafana or similar tools to visualize metrics like latency and throughput.

3. **Monitor Alerts**:

    - o Set thresholds to trigger alerts for issues like high error rates or slow responses.

Example Monitoring Workflow

Scenario: Monitor a customer support system deployed in the cloud.

Metrics Tracked:

1. **Request Latency**: Average time to respond to user queries.

2. **Error Rate**: Percentage of failed or incomplete workflows.

3. **CPU Utilization**: Ensure the system remains responsive under high load.

Implementation:

1. Configure LangFlow to export logs to CloudWatch.

2. Set up Grafana dashboards for visual insights.

3. Use alerts to notify the team of anomalies.

Expected Outcomes

By the end of this chapter, you will:

1. Understand deployment options for LangFlow workflows.

2. Be able to monitor and log deployed workflows for performance and reliability.

3. Ensure workflows operate efficiently and are scalable to meet user demands.

Deployment and monitoring are critical to ensuring LangFlow workflows deliver real-world impact, providing users with reliable, scalable, and high-performing AI applications.

Chapter 16: Collaborating with LangFlow

Collaboration is essential for teams working on LangFlow workflows, enabling shared development, improved productivity, and seamless knowledge transfer. This chapter explores strategies for version control, sharing workflows across teams, and creating comprehensive documentation with best practices to ensure smooth and effective collaboration.

16.1 Version Control for Workflows

Version control allows teams to track changes, revert to earlier states, and collaborate efficiently on workflows. Adopting version control practices ensures that multiple contributors can work on a project without conflict.

Why Use Version Control for Workflows?

1. **Change Tracking**:

   o   Record every modification to a workflow.

2. **Error Recovery**:

   o   Revert to a previous version if errors are introduced.

3. **Collaboration**:

   o   Enable multiple team members to work simultaneously.

4. **Accountability**:

   o   Identify who made specific changes and why.

Version Control with Git

Setting Up Git for LangFlow Workflows

1. **Initialize a Git Repository**:

   - Navigate to the folder containing LangFlow workflows and initialize Git.

bash

```
git init
```

2. **Add Workflow Files**:

   - Track workflow files (e.g., .json, .yaml).

bash

```
git add my_workflow.json
```

3. **Commit Changes**:

   - Save a snapshot of the current state.

bash

```
git commit -m "Initial commit of LangFlow workflow"
```

Example Workflow File Structure

c

```
langflow-project/
│
├── workflows/
│   ├── workflow1.json
│   ├── workflow2.json
│
├── docs/
```

```
|   ├── README.md
|   ├── workflow_guidelines.md
|
└── logs/
    ├── workflow_logs.log
```

Tracking Changes to Workflows

1. **Check Status**:

   o View modified files.

bash

git status

2. **View Differences**:

   o Compare changes between commits.

bash

git diff

Version Control Best Practices

Practice	Benefit
Use descriptive commit messages	Helps others understand the purpose of changes.
Create branches for features	Isolate work-in-progress changes.
Tag stable versions	Mark important milestones for release or deployment.

16.2 Sharing Workflows Across Teams

Sharing workflows ensures collaboration and consistency in large teams, enabling reusability and faster project development.

Methods for Sharing Workflows

1. File-Based Sharing

- Export workflows as .json or .yaml files.

- Share files through:

    - **Email**.

    - **Cloud Storage** (e.g., Google Drive, OneDrive).

2. Repository Sharing

- Use Git to share workflows via platforms like GitHub or GitLab.

    - Add team members as collaborators.

    - Use pull requests to review changes.

3. Workflow Management Tools

- Platforms like **Notion** or **Confluence** for centralized documentation.

- Dedicated LangFlow plugins for collaborative sharing.

Example: Sharing a Workflow on GitHub

Step 1: Create a Repository

1. Sign in to GitHub.

2. Click **New Repository**.

3. Upload workflow files.

Step 2: Add Team Members

1. Navigate to the **Settings** tab.

2. Select **Collaborators**.

3. Add team members via their GitHub usernames.

Step 3: Collaborate

1. Push updates to the repository:

bash

```
git push origin main
```

2. Team members pull changes:

bash

```
git pull origin main
```

Advantages of Team Collaboration

Advantage	Description
Centralized storage	Avoids scattered or outdated workflow versions.
Improved code quality	Team reviews improve accuracy and efficiency.
Faster problem-solving	Multiple perspectives accelerate issue resolution.

16.3 Documentation and Best Practices

Documentation is the cornerstone of effective collaboration. Comprehensive documentation helps team members understand workflows, maintain consistency, and onboard new contributors seamlessly.

Key Components of Workflow Documentation

1. Workflow Overview

- Purpose and objectives of the workflow.
- Key features or components.

2. Inputs and Outputs

- Describe expected inputs and generated outputs.
- Include example data for clarity.

3. Node Details

- Explain the purpose of each node.
- Highlight dependencies or configuration parameters.

4. Common Issues and Solutions

- Document known errors and troubleshooting steps.

5. Best Practices

- Guidelines for designing and maintaining workflows.

Example: Workflow Documentation Template

Workflow Name: Customer Support FAQ Automation
Purpose: Automatically answer FAQs using RAG.

Inputs:

Parameter Type Description

user_query   string Customer query for support.

Outputs:

Parameter   Type Description

response_text string Generated FAQ response.

Node Details:

Node Name   Purpose

Node Name	Purpose
Retrieval Node	Fetch relevant FAQs from the knowledge base.
LLM Node	Generate response based on retrieved content.

Common Issues:

Issue	Solution
Retrieval node timeout	Increase query timeout or optimize the database.

Best Practices for Documentation

Practice	Benefit
Use consistent formats	Ensures readability across teams.
Update regularly	Keeps documentation relevant and accurate.
Include visual aids	Diagrams or screenshots simplify complex workflows.

Tools for Documentation

Tool	Purpose
Markdown	Lightweight, easy-to-maintain documentation.
Notion	Collaborative documentation and workflow sharing.
Confluence	Centralized team documentation.

Expected Outcomes

By the end of this chapter, you will:

1. Implement version control for LangFlow workflows to track and manage changes.

2. Share workflows seamlessly across teams using file-based or repository methods.

3. Create and maintain detailed documentation for workflows, ensuring clarity and reusability.

Collaboration is a vital aspect of workflow development. With these strategies and best practices, teams can work together effectively, ensuring high-quality, consistent, and scalable LangFlow workflows.

Chapter 17: Workflow Design Best Practices

Designing workflows in LangFlow requires careful planning and execution to ensure scalability, efficiency, and reliability. This chapter explores best practices for modular workflow design, common pitfalls to avoid, and advanced tips to accelerate development, helping you create robust workflows ready for real-world deployment.

17.1 Modular Workflow Design for Scalability

Modular design is a cornerstone of scalable workflows. By breaking down workflows into independent, reusable components, you can improve flexibility, maintainability, and performance.

Key Principles of Modular Workflow Design

1. **Encapsulation:**
   - Each module or node should perform a single, well-defined task.

2. **Reusability:**
   - Design modules that can be reused across multiple workflows.

3. **Interoperability:**
   - Ensure that nodes can easily exchange data with one another.

4. **Separation of Concerns:**
   - Isolate logic into separate nodes to simplify debugging and updates.

Steps to Design Modular Workflows

1. Identify Core Functions

- Break down the workflow into discrete tasks (e.g., input processing, retrieval, generation).

2. Design Reusable Modules

- Create generic nodes for common tasks like data validation, summarization, or API calls.

3. Define Clear Input/Output Interfaces

- Standardize data formats passed between nodes to avoid compatibility issues.

4. Test Modules Independently

- Validate individual nodes before integrating them into larger workflows.

Example: Modular Workflow for Customer Support

Workflow Tasks:

1. Process user queries.

2. Retrieve relevant FAQ entries.

3. Generate a personalized response.

Modular Design:

Node Name	Purpose
Query Preprocessor	Cleans and validates user input.
FAQ Retrieval Node	Searches for relevant entries in a knowledge base.
Response Generator	Uses an LLM to create a response.

Benefits:

- Modules like **Query Preprocessor** can be reused in other workflows (e.g., chatbots or search engines).

Advantages of Modular Workflow Design

Advantage	Description
Scalability	Add or modify modules without affecting the entire workflow.
Maintainability	Easier to troubleshoot and update individual modules.
Reusability	Saves time by reusing existing components in new workflows.

17.2 Avoiding Common Pitfalls in LangFlow Development

Developing workflows in LangFlow can present challenges. Recognizing and avoiding common pitfalls ensures smoother development and deployment.

Common Pitfalls and Solutions

1. Poor Node Configuration

- **Problem**: Nodes are configured with incorrect parameters, leading to unexpected outputs.

- **Solution**: Double-check settings for each node and use descriptive names.

2. Lack of Error Handling

- **Problem**: Workflows fail when encountering unexpected inputs or external errors (e.g., API timeouts).

- **Solution**:

o   Add validation checks at input nodes.

o   Implement retry mechanisms for external calls.

3. Overcomplicated Workflows

- **Problem**: Complex workflows with too many interconnected nodes are hard to debug and scale.

- **Solution**:

    o   Use modular design to simplify workflows.

    o   Consolidate logic into fewer, more capable nodes.

4. Ignoring Performance Metrics

- **Problem**: Workflows are slow or resource-intensive, impacting usability.

- **Solution**:

    o   Monitor latency and throughput.

    o   Optimize frequently used nodes (e.g., caching API results).

5. Insufficient Testing

- **Problem**: Workflows fail in production due to edge cases missed during development.

- **Solution**:

    o   Test workflows with diverse inputs, including edge cases.

    o   Use automated tests to validate workflow logic.

Case Study: Troubleshooting a Broken Workflow

Scenario:

A workflow intended to summarize documents fails to return any results.

Troubleshooting Steps:

1. **Check Input Node**:

   o Verify that the document is properly uploaded and formatted.

2. **Validate Retrieval Node**:

   o Ensure the node successfully searches and retrieves data.

3. **Debug Generation Node**:

   o Test the LLM's prompt for errors or ambiguity.

4. **Solution**:

   o Adjust input formatting and refine the LLM's prompt to improve responses.

17.3 Pro Tips for Accelerating Development

Advanced techniques and best practices can help you build workflows more efficiently while maintaining high quality.

Pro Tips for Efficient Development

1. Use Templates

- **Tip**: Save frequently used workflows as templates.

- **Example**:

  o A pre-built FAQ workflow template can be adapted for different use cases with minor changes.

2. Leverage LangFlow Plugins

- **Tip**: Extend LangFlow's capabilities with plugins for custom tasks (e.g., sentiment analysis, advanced APIs).

- **Example**:

  o Integrate a plugin for multi-modal data processing.

3. Optimize Node Configuration

- **Tip**: Adjust node parameters like token limits and batch sizes for optimal performance.

- **Example**:

  - Reduce token usage in LLM nodes to minimize latency and cost.

4. Automate Testing

- **Tip**: Use testing frameworks to validate workflows automatically.

- **Example**:

  - Test different inputs and edge cases using a Python script.

Code Example:

python

```python
def test_workflow(workflow, test_cases):
    results = []
    for case in test_cases:
        result = workflow.run(case)
        results.append(result)
    return results

# Test cases
test_cases = ["What is AI?", "Explain blockchain.", "Benefits of LangFlow?"]
results = test_workflow(my_workflow, test_cases)
print(results)
```

Pro Tips for Collaboration

Tip	Benefit

Tip	Benefit
Use Git for version control	Enables seamless collaboration and rollback.
Document workflows thoroughly	Ensures clarity for all team members.
Standardize node naming conventions	Simplifies navigation in complex workflows.

Pro Tips for Performance Optimization

1. **Caching**:
   - Cache frequently retrieved data to reduce redundancy.

2. **Parallel Processing**:
   - Execute independent nodes simultaneously for faster execution.

3. **Data Preprocessing**:
   - Clean and format inputs before passing them to the workflow.

Example: Parallel Node Execution

Scenario:

Retrieve data from multiple APIs and process them in parallel.

Code Example:

python

```
import concurrent.futures

def fetch_api_1():
    # API call 1
```

```
    pass

def fetch_api_2():
    # API call 2
    pass

with concurrent.futures.ThreadPoolExecutor() as executor:
    results = list(executor.map(fetch_api, [fetch_api_1, fetch_api_2]))
```

Expected Outcomes

By the end of this chapter, you will:

1. Master modular workflow design for scalable and maintainable applications.

2. Identify and avoid common pitfalls in LangFlow development.

3. Apply advanced tips to accelerate development and enhance collaboration.

Adopting these best practices ensures that your LangFlow workflows are efficient, reliable, and ready for production, empowering you to create high-quality applications at scale.

Chapter 18: Future-Proofing LangFlow Applications

As LangFlow and its underlying framework, LangChain, continue to evolve, developers need to ensure that their workflows remain robust, scalable, and adaptable to new trends in AI. This chapter explores strategies for preparing workflows for updates in LangFlow and LangChain, and adapting them to leverage emerging trends in AI effectively.

18.1 Preparing for Updates in LangChain and LangFlow

Why Prepare for Updates?

Frequent updates in LangFlow and LangChain introduce new features, improve performance, and fix bugs. However, these changes can sometimes break existing workflows if not handled properly.

Key Challenges with Updates

Challenge	Impact
Deprecation of features	Breaks nodes or workflows relying on old APIs.
New dependency requirements	Causes compatibility issues with older environments.
Unforeseen behavioral changes	Alters the output or performance of workflows.

Strategies to Prepare for Updates

1. Stay Informed

- **Tip**: Regularly monitor release notes and update logs for LangFlow and LangChain.

- **Action**:

  - ○ Follow the LangFlow GitHub repository for updates.

  - ○ Subscribe to newsletters or forums related to LangFlow.

2. Use Semantic Versioning

- **Tip**: Understand versioning rules (e.g., MAJOR.MINOR.PATCH).

  - ○ **MAJOR**: Breaking changes.

  - ○ **MINOR**: New features, no breaking changes.

  - ○ **PATCH**: Bug fixes.

3. Test Updates in a Sandbox

- **Tip**: Use a staging environment to test updates before deploying them to production.

Example: Setting Up a Virtual Environment for Testing

bash

```
python -m venv langflow-test-env
source langflow-test-env/bin/activate
pip install langflow==latest
```

4. Modularize Workflows

- **Tip**: Break workflows into smaller, independent modules to isolate the impact of updates.

5. Maintain Backward Compatibility

- **Tip**: Use features and nodes with stable APIs.

- **Action**:

- o   Replace deprecated nodes or features as soon as possible.

6. Document Changes

- **Tip**: Keep a changelog to track workflow modifications due to updates.

    - o   **Example**: Note when a specific node was replaced or updated.

Example: Handling API Deprecation

Scenario: LangChain's text summarization API is deprecated.

Steps:

1. Identify the deprecated API from release notes.

2. Replace the old node with the new recommended feature.

3. Test the workflow to ensure consistency.

Code Example (Updating Summarization API):

python

```
# Old API
from langchain.text_splitter import RecursiveTextSplitter

# Updated API
from langchain.document_processors import TextSplitter

# Replace deprecated functionality
text_splitter = TextSplitter()
chunks = text_splitter.split_documents(long_text)
```

Tools for Managing Updates

Tool	Purpose
Git	Version control for managing workflow changes.
Docker	Containerization to test different LangFlow versions.
Changelogs	Documentation of workflow modifications.

18.2 Adapting Workflows for Emerging Trends in AI

Why Adapt to Trends?

The AI landscape evolves rapidly, introducing new technologies and methodologies. Adapting workflows to leverage these advancements ensures competitiveness and relevance.

Emerging Trends in AI and Their Impact on LangFlow

1. Multi-Modal Models

- **Description**: Models that handle text, images, audio, and more.

- **Impact**:
  - o Enable workflows to process and generate diverse data types.

- **Example**:
  - o Combine text queries with image analysis for advanced product search workflows.

Implementation in LangFlow:

1. **Input Node**: Accepts both text and images.

2. **Processing Node**: Uses a multi-modal model for analysis.

3. **Output Node**: Generates insights or recommendations.

Code Example:

python

```python
from transformers import BlipProcessor, BlipForConditionalGeneration
from PIL import Image

# Load multi-modal model
processor = BlipProcessor.from_pretrained("Salesforce/blip-image-captioning-base")
model = BlipForConditionalGeneration.from_pretrained("Salesforce/blip-image-captioning-base")

# Process input
image = Image.open("example.jpg")
inputs = processor(image, "Describe this image.", return_tensors="pt")

# Generate output
output = model.generate(**inputs)
print(processor.decode(output[0], skip_special_tokens=True))
```

---

2. Retrieval-Augmented Generation (RAG) 2.0

- **Description**: Enhanced RAG techniques with better knowledge retrieval mechanisms.

- **Impact**:
    - Improve the accuracy and relevance of generated content.

Adapting Workflows:

- Use advanced vector stores like Pinecone or Milvus.

- Integrate knowledge graphs for structured data retrieval.

---

3. Federated Learning

- **Description**: Train AI models on distributed datasets without centralizing data.

- **Impact**:

  - Enhance privacy in workflows handling sensitive data.

Example:

- Use federated learning for workflows involving healthcare or finance.

---

4. Real-Time AI

- **Description**: AI systems capable of processing and generating data in real time.

- **Impact**:

  - Enable workflows for dynamic environments like stock market analysis or real-time translation.

Implementation Tips:

- Optimize workflows for low-latency execution.

- Use asynchronous APIs and parallel processing.

Best Practices for Adapting to Trends

Practice	Benefit
Stay updated on AI research	Identify emerging trends early.

Practice	Benefit
Use flexible frameworks	Adapt workflows to new technologies seamlessly.
Experiment with prototypes	Validate new ideas before full-scale integration.

Case Study: Adapting to Multi-Modal Trends

Scenario:

A retail company wants to create a workflow that combines product images and user text queries to recommend items.

Workflow Design:

1. **Input Nodes**:
   - Accept product images and user descriptions.

2. **Processing Nodes**:
   - Use multi-modal AI to analyze image content and match it with textual descriptions.

3. **Retrieval Nodes**:
   - Query a product database for similar items.

4. **Output Node**:
   - Display recommendations.

Example Output:

- **Input**: Image of a red dress and the query, "Find something similar in blue."

- **Output**: "Recommended: Blue Summer Dress - $49.99."

Expected Outcomes

By the end of this chapter, you will:

1. Understand how to prepare LangFlow workflows for updates and changes in LangChain.

2. Adapt workflows to leverage emerging AI trends, ensuring relevance and scalability.

3. Implement best practices to future-proof LangFlow applications for long-term success.

Proactively preparing for updates and embracing new trends ensures your LangFlow applications remain innovative, effective, and resilient in the ever-evolving AI ecosystem.

Chapter 19: The Future of LangFlow

LangFlow is positioned at the intersection of cutting-edge AI technologies and practical workflow automation. As the field of AI continues to evolve, LangFlow's capabilities in agentic workflows and Retrieval-Augmented Generation (RAG) are poised to grow in relevance and influence. This chapter explores emerging trends in these domains and LangFlow's pivotal role in shaping the AI ecosystem.

19.1 Trends in Agentic Workflows and RAG
The Evolution of Agentic Workflows

What Are Agentic Workflows?

Agentic workflows are designed to mimic human-like decision-making, enabling autonomous agents to perform tasks such as:

1. Interacting with APIs.

2. Processing diverse data inputs.

3. Making decisions based on retrieved information.

Emerging Trends

1. **Multi-Agent Systems**:

    o **Trend**: Collaboration between multiple agents to handle complex, multi-step tasks.

    o **Example**:

        ▪ A customer service workflow where one agent retrieves FAQs, another identifies user sentiment, and a third generates the final response.

Implementation in LangFlow:

python

```
# Example of Multi-Agent System in LangFlow
from langchain.agents import Tool, initialize_agent
from langchain.llms import OpenAI

# Define tools for agents
tools = [
    Tool(name="FAQ Retrieval", func=faq_retrieval_function,
description="Retrieve FAQs"),
    Tool(name="Sentiment Analysis", func=sentiment_analysis_function,
description="Analyze user sentiment"),
]

# Initialize the multi-agent system
llm = OpenAI(model_name="gpt-3.5-turbo")
agent = initialize_agent(tools, llm, agent="zero-shot-react-description")

# Example query
result = agent.run("What is the refund policy for my recent order?")
print(result)
```

2. **Context-Aware Agents**:

   o **Trend**: Use of memory-enhanced agents that retain context across interactions.

   o **Example**:

      ▪ A conversational AI that remembers user preferences for personalized recommendations.

3. **Dynamic Workflow Adaptation**:

   o **Trend**: Real-time modification of workflows based on changing conditions.

   o **Example**:

- An e-commerce agent that adjusts its responses based on real-time inventory levels.

Advancements in Retrieval-Augmented Generation (RAG)

Why RAG Matters

RAG workflows combine knowledge retrieval with language generation to create highly accurate, context-aware outputs. This hybrid approach bridges the gap between static databases and dynamic AI generation.

Future Directions in RAG

1. **Knowledge Graph Integration**:

   - **Trend**: Use of structured knowledge graphs to enhance retrieval accuracy and semantic understanding.

   - **Example**:
     - Integrating Wikidata into a RAG workflow to improve question-answering capabilities.

2. **Neural Search Optimization**:

   - **Trend**: Leveraging advanced neural search algorithms for faster and more accurate retrieval.

   - **Example**:
     - Using dense vector representations with models like Sentence-BERT for efficient similarity searches.

Code Example:

python

```
from sentence_transformers import SentenceTransformer, util
```

```
# Load pre-trained model
model = SentenceTransformer('all-MiniLM-L6-v2')

# Example data
documents = ["AI ethics principles", "Deep learning applications", "AI in
healthcare"]
query = "What are the benefits of AI in medicine?"

# Compute embeddings
doc_embeddings = model.encode(documents, convert_to_tensor=True)
query_embedding = model.encode(query, convert_to_tensor=True)

# Find the most relevant document
scores = util.cos_sim(query_embedding, doc_embeddings)
best_doc_index = scores.argmax()
print(f"Best match: {documents[best_doc_index]}")
```

3. **Enhanced Multi-Modal RAG**:

   o **Trend**: Combining text, images, and other data
     modalities in retrieval workflows.

   o **Example**:

     ▪ An AI assistant that retrieves textual answers
       while analyzing visual data (e.g., product
       images).

4. **Scalable RAG Pipelines**:

   o **Trend**: Building pipelines that can handle large-
     scale, high-velocity queries.

   o **Example**:

     ▪ A news summarization system that retrieves
       and summarizes hundreds of articles daily.

Opportunities in Agentic Workflows and RAG

Opportunity	Description
Cross-Domain Applications	Apply workflows in finance, healthcare, and education.
Improved Human-AI Synergy	Combine automation with human oversight for critical tasks.
Real-Time Personalization	Use dynamic retrieval to tailor responses to individual users.

19.2 LangFlow's Role in the AI Ecosystem
The Growing Importance of LangFlow

LangFlow serves as a bridge between complex AI models and practical applications. By providing a visual interface for creating workflows, LangFlow democratizes AI development, empowering users of all skill levels.

Key Contributions of LangFlow

1. Simplifying Workflow Design

- LangFlow's drag-and-drop interface lowers the barrier to entry for non-technical users, enabling them to design sophisticated workflows without coding.

2. Enhancing Collaboration

- LangFlow facilitates team collaboration through shared workflows, version control, and centralized management.

3. Integrating Cutting-Edge AI Models

- LangFlow seamlessly incorporates state-of-the-art LLMs, vector stores, and other tools, ensuring users can leverage the latest advancements.

LangFlow in the Broader AI Ecosystem

Aspect	LangFlow's Role
Education	Providing an accessible platform for learning AI concepts.
Industry Applications	Accelerating the development of AI solutions in various sectors.
Research and Innovation	Supporting experimental workflows for academic and industrial R&D.

LangFlow's Roadmap and Future Goals

1. Advanced Multi-Modal Capabilities

- Expand support for audio, video, and multi-language inputs.

2. AI-Powered Workflow Suggestions

- Introduce intelligent recommendations for workflow design based on user goals.

3. Improved Performance

- Optimize execution speed and reduce latency for complex workflows.

4. Broader Integrations

- Add support for more third-party tools, APIs, and frameworks.

5. Community Growth

- Foster an open-source community to encourage contributions and innovation.

Case Study: LangFlow's Impact in Healthcare

Scenario:

A healthcare provider uses LangFlow to streamline patient triage.

Workflow:

1. **Input**: Patient symptoms and medical history.

2. **RAG System**: Retrieve relevant medical articles and guidelines.

3. **Decision Agent**: Recommend next steps (e.g., tests, referrals).

Outcome:

- Reduced wait times and improved diagnostic accuracy.

LangFlow's Potential for Societal Impact

1. **Accessibility**:

   o Lower costs and barriers for deploying AI solutions globally.

2. **Sustainability**:

   o Optimize workflows to minimize energy consumption in AI applications.

3. **Ethics**:

   o Promote transparency and accountability in AI-powered decisions.

Expected Outcomes

By the end of this chapter, you will:

1. Recognize emerging trends in agentic workflows and RAG and their potential applications.

2. Understand LangFlow's role as a critical tool in the AI ecosystem.

3. Be prepared to leverage LangFlow for future-proof, impactful AI solutions.

LangFlow stands as a versatile and powerful platform, ready to adapt to the rapidly changing landscape of AI and empower its users to build applications that are innovative, scalable, and transformative.

Chapter 20: Interactive Exercises

Practical exercises are an essential part of mastering LangFlow. This chapter provides hands-on activities that challenge you to build custom workflows, troubleshoot common errors, and optimize workflows for scalability. Each exercise includes clear instructions, detailed explanations, and examples to enhance your understanding and confidence in using LangFlow effectively.

20.1 Build a Custom Workflow with Agents and RAG

Objective

Create a workflow that combines agentic functionality with Retrieval-Augmented Generation (RAG) to answer user queries by retrieving information from a knowledge base and generating a coherent response.

Exercise Steps

Step 1: Define the Workflow Goal

- **Goal**: Build a workflow where:
    1. An **agent** interprets the user query.
    2. A **retrieval node** searches for relevant information.
    3. An **LLM node** generates the final answer.

Step 2: Prepare the Knowledge Base

- Use a sample knowledge base of FAQs or articles.
- **Example Data**:

plaintext

1. "LangFlow is a tool for designing workflows using AI."

2. "RAG combines retrieval and generation for accurate outputs."

3. "Agents in LangFlow automate decision-making tasks."

Step 3: Build the Workflow in LangFlow

1. **Input Node:**

   o Accepts a user query.

2. **Retrieval Node:**

   o Searches the knowledge base for relevant content.

3. **LLM Node:**

   o Synthesizes the retrieved data into a coherent response.

4. **Output Node:**

   o Displays the final answer.

Code Example

python

```python
from langchain.llms import OpenAI
from langchain.vectorstores import FAISS
from langchain.prompts import PromptTemplate

# Step 1: Create a vector store
documents = ["LangFlow is a tool for designing workflows using AI.",
        "RAG combines retrieval and generation for accurate outputs.",
        "Agents in LangFlow automate decision-making tasks."]
vector_store = FAISS.from_texts(documents)

# Step 2: Define the RAG workflow
def rag_workflow(query):
```

```
# Retrieve relevant documents
retrieved_docs = vector_store.similarity_search(query, top_k=2)
combined_text = " ".join([doc.page_content for doc in retrieved_docs])

# Generate a response
llm = OpenAI(model_name="gpt-3.5-turbo")
prompt = PromptTemplate(template="Use the following documents to answer
the query: {query}\n{docs}")
return llm.generate(prompt.format(query=query, docs=combined_text))

# Example query
response = rag_workflow("What is LangFlow?")
print(response)
```

Expected Outcome

- Input: "What is LangFlow?"

- Output: "LangFlow is a tool for designing workflows using AI."

20.2 Debugging Challenges: Troubleshooting Common Errors

Objective

Identify and resolve common errors in a LangFlow workflow.

Exercise: Debug a Broken Workflow

Scenario

You build a workflow to summarize documents, but it fails to return results.

Steps to Debug

Step 1: Check the Input Node

- **Error**: Input format is incorrect (e.g., missing fields).
- **Solution**:
  - Validate input data before processing.

Code Fix:

python

```
if not input_text:
    raise ValueError("Input text is missing.")
```

Step 2: Test the Retrieval Node

- **Error**: The retrieval node doesn't return relevant documents.
- **Solution**:
  - Ensure the vector store is correctly indexed.

Code Fix:

python

```
vector_store = FAISS.from_texts(documents)
if vector_store.is_empty():
    raise RuntimeError("Vector store is empty.")
```

Step 3: Refine the Prompt

- **Error**: The LLM generates irrelevant or incomplete answers.
- **Solution**:
  - Improve the prompt to provide clear instructions.

Improved Prompt:

plaintext

"Use the following information to summarize the key points:\n{docs}"

Step 4: Analyze Logs

- Use logging to identify where the workflow breaks.

Logging Example:

python

```
import logging

logging.basicConfig(level=logging.INFO)
logging.info("Starting workflow...")
```

Expected Outcome

- **Input**: Long document for summarization.
- **Output**: A coherent summary.

20.3 Optimize a Workflow for Scalability
Objective

Optimize a LangFlow workflow to handle large datasets and high traffic.

Exercise Steps

Step 1: Identify Bottlenecks

1. **Node Latency**:

   o Check which nodes take the longest to execute.

2. **Resource Usage**:

        o   Analyze CPU and memory consumption.

Step 2: Optimize the Workflow

1. Use Caching for Retrieval

- Cache frequently retrieved data to reduce redundant queries.

Code Example:

python

```python
from functools import lru_cache

@lru_cache(maxsize=100)
def cached_retrieval(query):
    return vector_store.similarity_search(query, top_k=3)
```

---

2. Parallelize Independent Nodes

- Process tasks in parallel where possible.

Code Example:

python

```python
import concurrent.futures

def process_node_1(data):
    # Simulate processing
    pass

def process_node_2(data):
    # Simulate processing
    pass

with concurrent.futures.ThreadPoolExecutor() as executor:
```

```
results = list(executor.map(process_node, [data_1, data_2]))
```

3. Reduce Token Usage in LLMs

- Limit input length to avoid exceeding token limits.

Code Example:

python

```
def truncate_text(text, max_tokens=300):
    return text[:max_tokens]
```

4. Scale with Cloud Resources

- Deploy the workflow on a cloud platform with auto-scaling enabled.

Testing Scalability

Scenario: Test the workflow with 1,000 queries.

Metrics to Monitor:

1. Latency (response time for each query).

2. Throughput (queries processed per second).

3. Error Rate (percentage of failed queries).

Expected Outcome

- **Before Optimization**:
  - Latency: 5 seconds/query
  - Throughput: 10 queries/second
- **After Optimization**:
  - Latency: 1 second/query

o   Throughput: 50 queries/second

Summary of Exercises

Exercise	Key Skill Developed
Build a Custom Workflow	Understand the integration of agents and RAG.
Debugging Challenges	Learn to troubleshoot and fix common errors.
Optimize a Workflow for Scalability	Enhance performance and handle large datasets.

By completing these exercises, you will gain hands-on experience in building, debugging, and optimizing LangFlow workflows. These practical skills are essential for designing scalable and reliable AI-powered solutions.

Chapter 21: Reference Materials

This chapter serves as a comprehensive reference guide to help you extend your learning and troubleshoot challenges in LangFlow and LangChain development. It includes essential documentation links, a glossary of terms, and a curated list of recommended tools, libraries, and resources.

21.1 LangFlow and LangChain Documentation
LangFlow Documentation

LangFlow provides extensive documentation to guide users in creating workflows, configuring nodes, and integrating external tools.

Key Sections

1. **Getting Started**:

   o Installation, basic configuration, and first workflow setup.

   o Example: Setting up LangFlow locally.

bash

pip install langflow
langflow --run example_workflow.json

2. **Node Descriptions**:

   o Detailed explanations of available nodes, including:

     ▪ Input nodes.

     ▪ Processing nodes.

     ▪ Output nodes.

   o Example: Using an LLM node to process text queries.

3. **Advanced Features**:

   o Integration with APIs, handling multi-modal data, and scaling workflows.

4. **Troubleshooting**:

   o Common issues and their resolutions.

Access LangFlow Documentation

- **Official Documentation**: LangFlow Docs

- **Community Forum**: Join discussions and find solutions to specific problems.

LangChain Documentation

LangChain is the foundational framework powering LangFlow. Understanding its core concepts enhances your ability to build and customize workflows.

Key Sections

1. **Components**:

   o LLMs: Setting up OpenAI, Hugging Face, or custom models.

   o Chains: Combining tasks into pipelines.

   o Agents: Dynamic tools for decision-making.

   o Memory: Context retention across interactions.

Example: Setting up a Hugging Face model in LangChain.

python

```
from langchain.llms import HuggingFaceHub
llm = HuggingFaceHub(repo_id="gpt-neo-2.7B")
```

2. **Integrations**:

- Working with APIs, vector stores (e.g., Pinecone), and knowledge bases.

3. **Use Cases**:

   - Tutorials and sample projects, such as RAG systems and multi-modal workflows.

4. **FAQ**:

   - Frequently asked questions and quick fixes for common issues.

Access LangChain Documentation

- **Official Documentation**: LangChain Docs

- **GitHub Repository**: LangChain GitHub

How to Use These Resources

1. **Beginner**: Start with LangFlow's "Getting Started" section.

2. **Intermediate**: Explore LangChain components to customize workflows.

3. **Advanced**: Dive into LangChain integrations for building cutting-edge applications.

21.2 Glossary of Terms and Key Concepts

This glossary provides concise definitions of essential terms and concepts in LangFlow and LangChain development.

Term	Definition
Agent	A dynamic AI entity that makes decisions or performs tasks based on inputs and available tools.
Node	A building block in LangFlow workflows, representing a specific function (e.g., input,

Term	Definition
	processing).
RAG (Retrieval-Augmented Generation)	Combines data retrieval with language generation for accurate, context-aware outputs.
LLM (Large Language Model)	AI models capable of processing and generating human-like text.
Memory	A feature that allows workflows to retain context across multiple interactions.
Vector Store	A database optimized for storing and querying embeddings, used in similarity searches.
Prompt Engineering	Crafting input prompts to guide the behavior of LLMs for specific outputs.
Multi-Modal Workflow	A workflow combining multiple data types (e.g., text, images) for richer functionality.
Semantic Search	A search technique using embeddings to find contextually relevant results.
Modular Design	Breaking workflows into independent, reusable components for scalability and maintainability.

21.3 Recommended Tools, Libraries, and Resources

Tools for Workflow Development

Tool	Purpose	Example Use Case

Tool	Purpose	Example Use Case
LangFlow	Visual tool for designing and managing AI workflows.	Build a FAQ bot with RAG.
LangChain	Python framework for constructing AI pipelines.	Integrate an LLM with a retrieval system.
Docker	Containerization for consistent deployment.	Deploy LangFlow workflows in a cloud environment.
VS Code	Lightweight IDE with extensions for Python and AI.	Edit and debug LangChain-based scripts.
Postman	API testing and integration.	Test API nodes in LangFlow workflows.

Libraries for AI and Data Processing

Library	Purpose	Example Use Case
Transformers (Hugging Face)	Access pre-trained language models.	Use GPT or T5 for text generation.
Pandas	Data manipulation and analysis.	Clean and preprocess data for workflows.
FAISS	Vector store for efficient similarity search.	Build a searchable knowledge base.
Django/Flask	Web frameworks for deploying LangFlow workflows.	Create a web app to host AI workflows.
Plotly	Data visualization and	Visualize workflow

Library	Purpose	Example Use Case
	dashboarding.	analytics.

Resources for Continuous Learning

Books

1. **"LangChain in Action"**:

   o A practical guide to building AI workflows with LangChain.

2. **"AI-Powered Workflows"**:

   o Strategies for integrating AI into business processes.

Online Courses

1. **LangFlow 101** (YouTube):

   o Free tutorials for beginners.

2. **Advanced LangChain** (Udemy):

   o Deep dives into LangChain components and integrations.

Communities

1. **LangFlow Discord**:

   o Connect with other developers for tips and troubleshooting.

2. **Stack Overflow**:

   o Search for solutions to common LangChain and LangFlow issues.

Newsletters

- **AI Workflow Weekly**:

    o Stay updated on the latest trends and tools in workflow automation.

How to Use Reference Materials Effectively

1. **For Problem-Solving**:
   - o Use documentation and forums to troubleshoot issues quickly.

2. **For Learning**:
   - o Explore books and courses to deepen your understanding.

3. **For Innovation**:
   - o Follow newsletters and communities to stay ahead of trends.

Expected Outcomes

By the end of this chapter, you will:

1. Know where to find official LangFlow and LangChain documentation for in-depth guidance.

2. Understand key terms and concepts through the glossary.

3. Have a curated list of tools, libraries, and resources to support your LangFlow development journey.

With these reference materials, you'll have everything you need to design, troubleshoot, and optimize AI workflows confidently and efficiently.

www.ingramcontent.com/pod-product-compliance
Lightning Source LLC
LaVergne TN
LVHW081528050326
832903LV00025B/1673